THE PATH TO GOD CONSCIOUSNESS.

Attend Spiritual Awakening, Get Inner
Peace and Serenity, Evolve Life Purpose,
and Greater Satisfaction and Fulfillment

Arun Kumara Khanda

https://arunkumarrk.com

YOUR FREE GIFT

As a token of my gratitude for taking out time to read my book, I would like to offer you a free gift. Click the below link or scan the QR code to download your free eBook PDF
https//arun-kumarkhanda.ck.page/00c46de54c

My Sincere Thanks

In my author journey, many blessings count toward my success. I am thankful to my mentor and bestselling author **Mr. Som Bathla** for mentoring, motivating, and guiding me to write, self-publish, and launch books on my way to the authopreneur journey. I am also thankful to my author community, especially Sooraj Achar, the bestselling author, for his timely technical support, encouragement, and advice to make my work easy. I am grateful to my readers for their support. I am happy to offer my gratitude to this Platform for the huge facilities given to the authors for transforming the lives of millions. Readers can connect with the author at akhanda1969@gmail.com

TABLE OF CONTENTS

Preface

In the vast tapestry of human existence, there exists an eternal quest—one that transcends the boundaries of time, culture, and individual belief systems. It is a journey toward a profound understanding, a connection that bridges the mortal with the divine. ***"Divine Connection: Exploring the Path to God Consciousness"*** embarks on this sacred odyssey, inviting seekers from all walks of life to traverse the inner landscapes of their being and unravel the mysteries that lie at the heart of existence.

Chapter One: Introduction

Our journey commences with an earnest invitation to ponder the profound significance of God Consciousness. This foundational chapter serves as a gateway, inviting readers to delve into the essence of our quest. We will unravel the intricate threads that intertwine spirituality and self-discovery, questioning the role of religion and exploring why it is imperative to seek a divine connection within the tapestry of our lives.

Chapter Two: What is God?

Venturing into the diverse beliefs surrounding the divine, the second chapter juxtaposes them against the lens of science. Together, we strive to comprehend the elusive nature of God, navigating the interplay between faith, spirituality, and the infinite perceptions that shape our understanding of the divine.

Chapter Three: The Importance of Self-Awareness

Our exploration moves inward, illuminating the profound relationship between self-awareness and God consciousness. Here, we provide practical tools to navigate the labyrinth of self-discovery, offering insights into overcoming obstacles that hinder our awareness and, consequently, impede our connection to the divine.

Chapter Four: Practices for Cultivating God Consciousness

Transitioning into the practical aspects of our journey, Chapter Four introduces a rich inventory of time-tested practices. From meditation to mindfulness, these serve as potent tools for cultivating a heightened awareness of the divine presence in our lives.

Chapter Five: The Role of Gratitude

In Chapter Five, we delve into the transformative power of gratitude, positioning it as a key that unlocks the gateway to God consciousness. We explore how a grateful heart can become a guiding beacon, leading us toward a more profound connection with the divine.

Chapter Six: The Power of Love

Celebrating the universal force of love, Chapter Six becomes a sanctuary where we explore its pivotal role in spiritual growth. Unraveling the intricacies of love, we navigate its manifestations from self-love to compassion for others, understanding it as a catalyst for transcending spiritual boundaries.

Chapter Seven: Overcoming Obstacles to God Consciousness

No transformative journey is without challenges. Chapter seven identifies common obstacles to spiritual growth and offers strategies to overcome them. It ensures that seekers remain motivated on the path to God consciousness, equipped with the tools to navigate the hurdles they may encounter.

Chapter Eight: The Importance of Community

Recognizing the strength found in unity, Chapter 8 explores the role of community in spiritual growth. It guides readers in finding supportive communities and provides insights into navigating the challenges inherent within them.

Chapter Nine: Living a God-Conscious Life

Practical integration takes center stage in Chapter 9, where we delve into the art of weaving spiritual practices into the fabric of daily life. Exploring the nuances of maintaining a connection with the divine amidst life's myriad challenges, this chapter serves as a guide for practical application.

Chapter Ten: Conclusion

Our journey concludes with reflections on the profound odyssey undertaken. Chapter 10 serves as a contemplative space, encouraging readers to reflect on the transformative path to God consciousness and offering insights into future steps on this infinite journey.

As we embark on this exploration, let this book serve as a guide, a companion, and a source of inspiration for those seeking to unravel the profound mysteries of existence and forge an unbreakable connection with the divine. May this journey be transformative, enlightening, and, above all, deeply enriching. Onward, fellow seekers, to the heart of God consciousness.

Chapter One

Introduction

"I believe in God, but not as one thing, not as an old man in the sky. I believe that what people call God is something in All of us. I believe that what Jesus and Mohammed and Buddha and All the rest said was right. It's just that the translations have gone wrong."-John Lennon

Defining God Consciousness

God consciousness refers to a state of awareness or realization in which an individual perceives and experiences a profound connection with the supernatural power known as divine. Divine or ultimate reality, often referred to as God, the Supreme Being, or the Source or the highest positive energy. It is a concept that transcends religious and cultural boundaries and is found in various spiritual traditions around the world. One can't perceive the true essence of the Supreme Being by his ordinary sense organs and it needs something special beyond the same.

"God is the creator. Everything in our world, everything we see, hear, taste, smell, and touch; every thought, feeling, fantasy, intimation, hope, and fear; it is all a form that consciousness has taken on."-Deepak Chopra

The specific understanding and interpretation of God consciousness may vary among different belief systems. *However, it generally involves an expanded sense of self, a deep recognition of an interconnectedness with all of creation, and a heightened awareness of the divine presence within, and around us.* Let us together explore some key aspects that can help define God-consciousness.

Unity and Interconnectedness

God consciousness acknowledges the fundamental unity and interconnectedness of all existence. It recognizes that all beings and phenomena are ultimately interconnected and arise from the same source. In the Bhagavad Gita, there is a specific verse where Lord Krishna explicitly states that everything is made by Him. One such verse is:

अहं सर्वस्य प्रभवो मत्तः सर्वं प्रवर्तते।

इति मत्वा भजन्ते मां बुधा भावसमन्विताः॥ गीता ॥ 10.8 ॥

aham sarvasya prabhavo mattaḥ sarvam pravartate
iti matvā bhajante mām budhā bhāva-samanvitāḥ.

"I am the source of all spiritual and material worlds. Everything emanates from Me. The wise who know this perfectly engage in My devotional service and worship Me with all their hearts."

This verse emphasizes that Lord Krishna is the origin of everything, both spiritual and material. All things manifest from Him, and He sustains the entire creation. The wise who understand this truth worship Him with devotion and love.

Bible says-Psalm 46:10 (New International Version):

"Be still, and know that I am God;

I will be exalted among the nations,

I will be exalted in the earth."

This verse reminds us to find inner stillness and acknowledge the presence of God. It emphasizes that the Divine is in control and will be exalted and recognized throughout the world. This understanding leads to a sense of oneness and a dissolution of perceived boundaries between oneself and others.

"God consciousness is the awareness of the divine presence within oneself and in all of creation." -Paramahansa Yogananda:

Transcendence of Ego

God consciousness involves transcending the limitations of the ego, which is the sense of individual identity and separation. It goes beyond the identification with the physical body, personal desires, and attachments, allowing for a broader perspective that encompasses the entire universe. We can understand better if we observe the famous quote of a famous Indian monk and philosopher.

"To attain God consciousness, one must transcend the limitations of the ego and merge

with the universal consciousness."- Swami Vivekananda

Divine Presence

God consciousness involves a heightened awareness of the divine presence that permeates everything. It recognizes that the divine is not only present in specific religious symbols, places, or rituals but ***is omnipresent and can be experienced directly within oneself and in every aspect of life.***

In the Bhagavad Gita, the concept of non-separation between the individual self (Atman) and the Divine (Brahman) is described in various verses. One of the significant verses that expresses this idea is:

यो मां पश्यति सर्वत्र सर्वं च मयि पश्यति।

तस्याहं न प्रणश्यामि स च मे न प्रणश्यति॥ गीता ॥ 6.30 ॥

yo māṁ paśyati sarvatra sarvaṁ ca mayi paśyati
tasyāhaṁ na praṇaśyāmi sa ca me na praṇaśyati

"For one who sees Me everywhere and sees everything in Me, I am never lost, nor is he ever lost to Me."

In this verse, Lord Krishna explains that the one who perceives the Divine (Himself) in everything and sees everything within the Divine never becomes separated from Him (Divine). It highlights the idea of unity and interconnectedness between the individual soul (Atman) and the Supreme Soul (Brahman).

"In God consciousness, there is no separation between the self and the divine. It is the realization that we are all interconnected and part of a greater whole." Eckhart Tolle:

Love and Compassion

God consciousness is often accompanied by an overwhelming sense of love, compassion, and empathy toward all beings. It arises from the recognition that the divine essence resides within every living and non-living being and fosters deep care for the well-being of others. In Hindu philosophy, it is believed the divine presence in living animals is *Chetan* (active), living trees and plants, etc. as *Ardha-Chetan* (half active), and within non-living things as *Achetana* (inactive).

We may cite a relevant quote from *Swami Vivekananda* ***"The moment I realized God sitting in the temple of every human body, the moment I stand in reverence before every human being and see God in him-that moment I am free from bondage, everything that binds vanishes, and I am free."*** This is one of the best examples of God realization. God realization needs a definite framework of the spiritual mind of compassion, kindness, and inner farsightedness.

Expanded Consciousness

In the state of God consciousness, there is a shift from the ordinary, limited consciousness to an expanded state of awareness and unlimited bliss. *It involves a profound sense of clarity, wisdom, and insight that goes beyond intellectual understanding and taps into deeper truth and knowing.* That stage can't be expressed in words but can only be realized ***by the selfless self***.

Transcendence of Duality

God consciousness moves beyond the perception of reality as a dualistic interplay of opposites (such as good vs. evil, right vs. wrong). Instead, it embraces a holistic perspective that recognizes the underlying unity and harmony behind apparent contradictions.

Bliss and Joy

God consciousness is often accompanied by a deep sense of bliss, joy, happiness, and peace that transcends external circumstances. This inner state of well-being arises from the realization of **one's inherent connection with the divine and the alignment of one's life with spiritual values.**

It's important to note that God consciousness is **a deeply personal and subjective experience**. It may be pursued through various spiritual practices such **as meditation, prayer, contemplation, and self-inquiry.** Different individuals may have unique paths and experiences on their journey toward realizing and embodying God consciousness.

Why it's Important to Seek a Divine Connection

Divine generally refers to something that is related to a deity or a higher unseen power. It can be used to describe qualities, actions, or phenomena that are considered sacred, holy, or associated with the divine realm. It is something magical that is beyond the power of the human being and celebrated by the so-called wise people of the universe. It is supreme and kind that leads to happiness and at the same time ultimate truth. The term **"divine"** is often used in religious or spiritual contexts to describe the nature of gods, goddesses, or the transcendent.

A divine connection, on the other hand, refers to a relationship or bond between an individual and the divine or higher power. It implies a sense of communion, closeness, or communication with the divine realm. People who believe in divine connections often perceive themselves as being spiritually linked or in tune with the divine, allowing them to experience a heightened sense of guidance, purpose, or spiritual energy.

The nature of divine connections varies across different religious and spiritual beliefs. It may also differ in personal perspectives. *Some may view it as a personal experience of connecting with a specific deity or a universal divine energy. Others may describe it as an intuitive awareness of being connected to something greater than oneself or as a form of spiritual awakening.*

Seeking a divine connection or cultivating a relationship with the divine is important for several reasons. Here are some key points that highlight the significance of seeking a divine connection:

Spiritual Fulfillment

Seeking a divine connection provides a sense of spiritual fulfillment and nourishment. As human beings, we have an innate longing for meaning, purpose, and transcendence. A connection with the divine can satisfy this deep longing, offering a sense of wholeness, peace, and inner fulfillment. It is believed that without divine connection human life is at par beast. Every animal has four inseparable needs *Aahara*(food), *Nidra* (Sleep), *Bhaya* (fear), and *Maithuna*(sex). One special aspect of humans that makes them unique is their conscience, search for the true self, quest for knowledge, and enlightenment. The enlightenment comes from divine connection, which leads to spiritual fulfillment.

Guidance and Direction

A divine connection can provide guidance and direction in life. By establishing a relationship with the divine, we open ourselves to receiving insights, inspiration, and wisdom that can help us navigate through challenges, make important decisions, and find our true path—the path to peace, joy, and fulfillment.

Source of Love and Support

Connecting with the divine can offer a source of unconditional love, support, and comfort. It allows us to experience a deep sense of being cared for, accepted, and cherished. ***This connection can provide solace during difficult times, offering strength and resilience to overcome obstacles.*** Divine support which is called God is considered everything for the man connected. A universal Vedic prayer is-

तोमेब माता च पिता तोमेब।
तोमेब बन्धु च सखा तोमेब।
तोमेब विद्या द्रविणं तोमेब।
तोमेब सर्वं मम देवदेव॥

tomeba mātā cha pitā tomeba
tomeba bandhu cha sakhā tomeba
tomeba vidyā draviṇaṁ tomeba
tomeba sarvaṁ mama devadeva

You (God/Divine) are my mother and you are my father. You are my relative and you are my friend. You are knowledge and you are wealth. You are everything, my divine Lord. The prayer can be directed to any divine entity, any God, Goddess, any image, any form or formless supreme power or energy. He is present everywhere, as ***Bhagavad*** Gita says;

सर्वतः पाणिपादं तत्सर्वतोऽक्षिशिरोमुखम्।
सर्वतः श्रुतिमल्लोके सर्वमावृत्य तिष्ठति॥ गीता ॥13.13॥

sarvataḥ pāṇipādaṁ tatsarvato'kṣiśiromukham
sarvataḥ śrutimalloke sarvam āvṛtya tiṣṭhati.

"Everywhere are His hands and feet, His eyes, heads, and faces. His ears are everywhere, and He pervades everything in the universe. In this way, the Supreme Soul exists, entering and covering everything in the world."

In this verse, Lord Krishna describes the omnipresence of the Supreme Soul (*Paramatma*), illustrating that the Divine's hands, feet, eyes, heads, and faces are present everywhere. The Divine pervades all of creation, encompassing and overseeing everything in the universe.

Moral and Ethical Framework

A divine connection often leads to the development of a moral and ethical framework in the mind of the individual. Many spiritual traditions emphasize virtues such as **compassion, kindness, forgiveness, and integrity.** By cultivating a connection with the divine, we align ourselves with these values and strive to live a life that is guided by principles that promote harmony, justice, and the well-being of all beings.

Upanishad says-

सर्वे भवन्तु सुखिनः, सर्वे सन्तु निरामयाः।
सर्वे भद्राणि पश्यन्तु, मा कश्चित् दुःखभाग्भवेत्॥

May all beings find happiness,
may all beings enjoy good health,

May all witness prosperity,
may none endure suffering.

These universal wishes of compassion and goodwill have their origins in the sacred land of India, where sages and Rishis bestowed them upon us.

Expanded Awareness and Consciousness

Seeking a divine connection expands our awareness and consciousness. ***It helps us transcend limited perspectives and opens us to a broader understanding of reality***. This expanded awareness allows us to see beyond *the **superficial aspects of life** and recognize **the inner values, the real purpose of life,*** and the interconnectedness of all existence. It leads the humans to path of enlightenment and living an awakened purposeful divine life. The expanded awareness harnesses the power of a bigger understanding of the universe, the living and non-living beings, and overall, ourselves. Our ego and superego are understood along with our understanding of self.

Transformation and Growth

A divine connection can be a catalyst for personal transformation and growth. It supports us in releasing limiting beliefs, patterns, and attachments, enabling us to evolve into our highest potential. This process of spiritual growth fosters self-awareness, self-realization, and *the **development of virtues and qualities that lead to a more fulfilling and purposeful limitless life.***

Connection with Something Greater

Seeking a divine connection allows us to connect with something greater than ourselves. It helps us **transcend** the ego-driven mindset and opens us to a broader perspective that recognizes the interplay of forces beyond the physical realm. This connection offers a sense of **awe, wonder, and reverence for the vastness and mystery of existence.**

Ultimately, the importance of seeking a divine connection lies in the deepening of our relationship with the sacred and the exploration of our spiritual nature. It provides a means to cultivate inner peace, find meaning and purpose, and contribute positively to the world around us.

Role of Religion in God Consciousness

"Religion is the belief in the existence of a power that human beings cannot comprehend, that is directing their lives and the world around them." - Albert Einstein

This quote provides insights into how religion is perceived as a response to the mysteries of existence and the profound questions that humans encounter in their journey through life. The role of religion in the journey to God consciousness is significant for many individuals. However, it can vary depending on personal beliefs, social-cultural backing, upbringing, and experiences. Here are some key aspects of the role of religion in God consciousness:

Framework for Spiritual Practice

Religion often provides a structured framework for spiritual practice. It offers, rituals, prayers, and specific guidelines that help individuals connect with the divine. These practices can serve as a pathway to deepen one's spiritual awareness and foster a sense of devotion and reverence. For this purpose, different festivals and cultural gatherings are systematically annexed into social lives.

Moral and Ethical Guidance

Religions often provide moral and ethical principles that guide individuals in their actions and choices. These teachings help shape one's character and behavior, encouraging qualities such as compassion, honesty, kindness, and justice. The religious scriptures and teachings can support the development of virtues and align one's actions with the divine will. Some quotes from different belief systems highlight the same.

Christianity: "So whatever you wish that others would do to you, do to them, for this is the law and the prophets." (Matthew 7:12)

Islam: "The believers are nothing but brothers and sisters, so make peace between your two brothers [or sisters]; and fear Allah, perhaps you will be shown mercy." (Quran 49:10)

Hinduism: "This is the supreme secret: treat all beings as you would treat yourself." (Manusmriti 12.125)

Buddhism: "Hurt not others with that which hurts yourself." (Dhammapada 137)

Judaism: "Therefore you shall keep my statutes and my ordinances, for whoever does them will live by them: I am the Lord." (Leviticus 18:5)

Community and Support

Religion provides a sense of community and belonging. It brings people together who share similar beliefs, values, and spiritual aspirations. This community can offer support, encouragement, and a sense of connection during the journey to God consciousness. ***Religious gatherings, ceremonies, and group practices provide opportunities for communal worship, reflection, and spiritual growth.***

Sacred Texts and Teachings

Religious traditions often have sacred texts and teachings that contain profound wisdom, spiritual insights, and stories that inspire individuals on their path. These texts can serve as **a source of guidance, inspiration, and contemplation**, offering deep insights into the nature of the divine and providing a roadmap for spiritual growth. ***The Bible, The Shrimad Bhagavad Gita, The Ramayana, The Qur'an, The Guru Granth Sahib, The Hebrew Bible, The Tripitaka, Agamas, The Vedas,*** etc.

are a few examples of sacred texts of different religious faiths and belief systems.

Spiritual Guidance and Leadership

Religious traditions often have spiritual leaders, such as ***priests, pastors, rabbis, spiritual teachers, saints, and gurus*** who provide guidance, support, and interpretation of religious teachings. These leaders can serve as mentors and sources of wisdom, helping individuals navigate the complexities of their spiritual journey and offering insights on attaining God consciousness. The Role of Gurus, spiritual teachers, or spiritual leaders in shaping true ethical values and guidance is recognized. ***The real self-realized Guru or spiritual leaders are in true sense flag bearers of God consciousness and guides of their disciples.*** In a real sense, they are the assets of the universe and Godly. No language or literature can define their true values and services rendered to human society in uplifting spiritual ethics and creating awareness within humanism.

Rituals and Symbolism

Religious rituals and symbolism can serve as powerful tools for connecting with the divine. They provide tangible expressions of devotion, worship, and reverence. These rituals can create a sacred space and time for individuals to engage in acts of ***prayer, meditation, recitation of mantras (code name of God), and contemplation,*** deepening their connection with the divine.

Cultural and Historical Context

Religion is often deeply intertwined with cultural and historical contexts. It can provide a rich tapestry of traditions, customs, and practices that connect individuals to their heritage and provide a sense of continuity with the past. This cultural and historical context can deepen one's understanding of spirituality and contribute to a sense of identity and belonging. Without the rich tradition and cultural heritage human civilization is not fulfilled in itself. They are the essence of human belief systems and they are inherited for generations. Hindu civilization, culture, and religion can't exist without the deities of God, goddesses, temples, and the festivals associated with it. Similarly, without the institution of church and masjid Christianity and Muslim religious traditions and belief systems can't exist respectively.

Inspiration and Hope

Religion often offers narratives and teachings that inspire hope, faith, and resilience in the face of challenges. It provides a sense of purpose and meaning in life, as well as a belief in the ultimate goodness and benevolence of the divine. This inspiration and hope can sustain individuals on their journey to God consciousness, especially during difficult times.

It's important to note that *while religion can be a powerful vehicle for spiritual growth and the path to God-consciousness for many, it is not the only path. Some individuals may find their spiritual connection and awakening outside the confines of organized religion.* The journey to God consciousness is deeply personal, and different paths can lead to the same destination. Ultimately, it is about finding an authentic connection with the divine that resonates with your own beliefs, experiences, and inner guidance.

Spirituality and God Consciousness

"Spiritual knowledge is the only thing that can destroy our miseries forever, any other knowledge satisfies wants only for a time. It is only with the knowledge of the spirit that the faculty of want is annihilated forever; so helping man spiritually is the highest help that can be given to him. He who gives man spiritual knowledge is the greatest benefactor of mankind and we always find that those were the most powerful of men who helped man in his spiritual needs because spirituality is the true basis of all our activities in life."-Swami Vivekananda

Spirituality and God-consciousness are closely related concepts, but they have distinct meanings. Here's an explanation of each:

Spirituality:

Spirituality refers to the exploration and expression of the spiritual aspects of human existence. It encompasses a broad range of beliefs, practices, and experiences that involve connecting with something greater than oneself, seeking meaning and purpose in life, and exploring the nature of reality beyond the physical realm.

"The spiritual journey is individual, highly personal. It can't be organized or regulated. It isn't true that everyone should follow one path. Listen to your truth."-Ram Dass

Spirituality is a deeply personal and subjective experience, as it involves an individual's quest for transcendence, inner peace, and a sense of connectedness to the universe. It can be pursued within or outside the framework of organized religion, and it is not limited to any particular faith or belief system.

Spirituality often involves practices such as meditation, recitation of the name of God, (reciting the guru mantra) prayer, contemplation, mindfulness, self-reflection, and engaging with nature. It emphasizes the development of virtues, self-awareness, compassion, and a deepening understanding of oneself and the world. Spirituality encourages individuals to explore the depths of their being, connect with their inner wisdom, and align their thoughts, actions, and values with their higher self or a transcendent reality.

God Consciousness

God consciousness refers to a state of heightened awareness and connection with the divine or a higher power. It is an experiential realization and recognition of the presence of the divine in oneself, others, and the world. *God consciousness involves transcending the limited egoist self and perceiving the underlying unity, love, and wisdom that permeate all of creation.*

In the state of God consciousness, one experiences a deep sense of interconnectedness, unconditional love, and a profound understanding of the nature of reality. ***It goes beyond intellectual belief or religious dogma and involves a direct experiential knowing of the divine***. This state of consciousness can be attained through various spiritual practices, deep meditation, mystical experiences, or moments of profound insight and awakening. In Hinduism, one of the best ways to God consciousness is called ***Bhakti.***

Bhakti, in the context of Hinduism, is a central and widely practiced spiritual concept that refers to a deep and loving devotion to a chosen deity or form of the divine. It is considered one of the major paths to spiritual realization and liberation (moksha) in Hindu philosophy.

The word *"bhakti"* is derived from the Sanskrit root *"bhaj,"* which means to adore, worship, or serve. ***Bhakti involves a heartfelt and intense emotional connection with the divine, characterized by love, surrender, and selfless devotion***. It transcends mere ritualistic practices and formalities, emphasizing a personal and intimate relationship between the devotee *(bhakta)* and the divine (*Bhagaban*). The bhakti can be navadha or nine types, such as *dashya, sakhya, batsalya, prema,* or *kanta, etc.*

Key Aspects of Bhakti in Hinduism

1. Love and Devotion: Bhakti is primarily about cultivating a deep sense of love, affection, and devotion toward the chosen deity or god. This love is expressed through prayers, kirtan, hymns, chanting, singing bhajans (devotional songs), and performing rituals dedicated to the deity.

2. Surrender and Faith: Bhakti involves the complete surrender of the self to the divine, acknowledging the supreme power and wisdom of the chosen deity. The devotee places unwavering faith in the deity's grace and protection.

3. Personalization of the Divine: Unlike some other spiritual paths, Bhakti encourages a personalized approach to the divine. Devotees often perceive the divine as a loving and compassionate friend, parent, or beloved, with whom they can communicate on an emotional level.

4. Service and Compassion: Bhakti emphasizes selfless service (*seva*) to the deity. It also emphasizes the concept of "service to mankind is service to god" seeing the divine presence in all living beings. Acts of kindness, charity, and compassion are considered important expressions of devotion.

5. Detachment from Worldly Desires: While devotion and love are central to Bhakti, it also teaches detachment from material desires and ego, focusing on spiritual growth and inner transformation.

Bhakti is not limited to any specific form of the divine, and Hindus can choose to practice it through devotion to various deities like Vishnu, Shiva, Durga, Krishna, Rama, or others. Throughout history, Bhakti has been instrumental in inspiring saints, poets, and devotees who expressed their love and devotion through a rich tapestry of literature, art, and cultural practices.

God Consciousness in Christianity

Jesus Christ holds a central role in Christian theology, serving as the intermediary between humanity and God. His life and teachings serve as a blueprint for living in alignment with God, emphasizing principles such as prayer, love, forgiveness, and self-sacrifice.

To foster a sense of God-consciousness, various Christian traditions advocate specific practices, including:

1. *Prayer and Contemplation:* Regularly setting aside time for prayer and silent reflection fosters a deeper connection with the divine.

2. *Scripture Exploration:* Engaging in the study of the Bible provides valuable insights into God's nature and His intended path for individuals.

3. *Sacraments and Worship:* Active participation in religious rituals and ceremonies creates communal experiences that facilitate encounters with the divine.

4. *Service and Compassion*: Living out God's teachings involves selfless acts of service to others, driven by love

and empathy. Such actions become expressions of one's awareness and connection with God.

God consciousness can be understood in different ways, depending on one's beliefs and spiritual awakening path. It can be seen as merging with a personal God, connecting with a universal consciousness, or realizing one's divine essence. It is an ongoing journey of deepening awareness, growth, and alignment with the divine.

While spirituality encompasses a broader range of experiences and beliefs, God consciousness specifically refers to a heightened state of awareness and connection with the divine. However, it's important to note that the exact terminology and interpretations may vary across different religious and spiritual traditions.

Ultimately, spirituality and God-consciousness are intertwined in the exploration of the deeper dimensions of human existence and the quest for a profound connection with the divine or transcendent aspects of reality. They are deeply personal and can lead to profound transformation, inner fulfillment, and a sense of a bigger purpose in life.

Chapter Two

What is God?

"God is the friend of silence. See how nature - trees, flowers, grass - grows in silence; see the stars, the moon, and the sun, how they move in silence... We need silence to be able to touch souls." - Mother Teresa

"God is not a person. God is not a thing. God is the eternal dance of energy, the infinite ocean of potentiality, the source of all that is." - *Deepak Chopra*

Different Beliefs About God

God is a mystery, a concept of realization, an ocean of cosmic consciousness and absolute truth. We the human being can't describe Him with our manly voice and language. Because He is beyond our thought, imagination, perception, knowledge, power, and whatever quality we have to ascertain Him. The grate bhakta/devotee friend of Lord Krishna Arjun proclaimed about Him;

स्वयमेवात्मनात्मानं वेत्थ त्वं पुरुषोत्तम।

भूतभावन भूतेश देवदेव जगत्पते॥ गीता II 10.15 II

svayamevātmanātmānaṁ vettha tvaṁ puruṣottama
bhūta-bhāvana bhūteśa devadeva jagatpate.

*"You alone know yourself by yourself, O Supreme
Person, O Source of all beings, O Lord of the universe,
O God of gods, O Ruler of the world!"*

In this verse, Arjun acknowledges Lord Krishna as the
Supreme Being, after he became conscious of Krishna as
the Ultimate Reality and the Source of all creation.
Arjun realizes that only Krishna Himself fully knows His
divine nature and the vastness of His existence. The
verse expresses Arjun's reverence and recognition of
Krishna's divine sovereignty and omniscience.

Different beliefs about God vary across cultures,
traditions, religions, and individual philosophies. Here
are some examples of different beliefs about God:

Monotheism

Monotheistic belief systems believe in a singular,
supreme deity who is omnipotent (all-powerful),
omniscient (all-knowing), and omnipresent (present
everywhere). Monotheistic traditions emphasize the
unity and oneness of God.

Let us see a few examples of religions that embrace
monotheism:

Judaism

Judaism is one of the oldest monotheistic religions, dating back thousands of years. It holds that there is only one God, *Yahweh*. Yahweh is also known as **Adonai** or **Elohim,** which are Hebrew words for "Lord" and "God," respectively. Due to the holy nature of Yahweh's name, Jews traditionally avoid pronouncing it directly and often use substitutes like **"Adonai" or "HaShem"**. Jews believe that Yahweh is the creator of the universe and the God of Abraham, Isaac, and Jacob. They also believe that Yahweh gave the *Torah*, or *Hebrew Bible*, to Moses on Mount Sinai.

Christianity

Christianity, originating from Judaism, also professes belief in one God. Christians believe in the Holy Trinity, comprising **God** the Father, **Jesus Christ** (God's Son), and the **Holy Spirit**, as three distinct yet unified aspects of the one God.

Islam

Islam is another prominent monotheistic religion. Muslims believe in one God, **Allah,** who revealed himself through the **Prophet Muhammad**. The Islamic faith emphasizes the unity and transcendence of Allah and acknowledges Muhammad as the final prophet.

Sikhism

Sikhism, founded in the 15th century in Punjab, India, is a monotheistic religion that follows the teachings of Guru Nanak Dev Ji and subsequent Sikh Gurus. Sikhs believe in the existence of one Supreme Being, *Ik Onkar*, who is formless and without gender. The name of the God of Sikhism is also known as *Waheguru,* which means *"Wonderful Enlightener."* He is the creator, sustainer, and destroyer of the universe. God is described as being all-powerful, all-knowing, and all-merciful.

Sikhs believe that God is present in all of creation and that all beings are equal in the eyes of God. They also believe that God is a personal God who can be communicated with through prayer and meditation.

Baha'i Faith: The Baha'i Faith, established in the 19th century, promotes the belief in one God who is unknowable and beyond human comprehension. Baha'is believe that God has sent various messengers, including **Baha'u'llah,** to guide humanity throughout history.

A sect of the Hindu religion called *Advaita* also believes in the same philosophy of *the* oneness of God. These religions exemplify monotheism by affirming the existence of a single, all-powerful deity while expressing diverse beliefs and practices within their respective traditions.

Polytheism

Polytheistic belief systems, found in ancient religions like *Greek mythology and Hinduism*, believe in the existence of multiple gods and goddesses. Each deity is associated with specific domains or aspects of life and can be worshipped individually or collectively. Zeus (Jupiter, in Roman mythology): the king of all Gods, the god of wealth, law, and fate. Poseidon, Hera (Juno): the queen of the gods and goddess of women and marriage, Hestia and Demeter, Hades, are the mythical gods of Greek mythology. Later on, Apollo: God of prophecy, music poetry, and knowledge, Artemis, Hermes, Athena, Hephaestus, Aphrodite (Venus): goddess of beauty and love, and Ares were added to the Greek pantheon.

Likely in Hindu mythology three principal Gods Brahma, the creator of the universe, Vishnu nurture, protect, and preserve the creations and Maheswar, the destroyer of the creation. The goddesses Sabitri, Mahalaxmi, and Parvati respectively are recognized as the consorts of Brahma, Vishnu, and Maheswar with separate domains.

Krishna an incarnation of Lord Vishnu declares in **The Bhagavad Gita** His mission for incarnations.

यदा यदा हि धर्मस्य ग्लानिर्भवति भारत।

अभ्युत्थानमधर्मस्य तदात्मानं सृजाम्यहम्॥

परित्राणाय साधूनां विनाशाय च दुष्कृताम्।

धर्मसंस्थापनार्थाय सम्भवामि युगे युगे॥   गीता ॥ 4.7, 8 ॥

Yadā yadā hi dharmasya glānir bhavati bhārata
Abhyutthānam adharmasya tadātmānaṁ sṛjāmyaham
Paritrāṇāya sādhūnāṁ vināśāya cha duṣkṛtām
Dharma-saṁsthāpanārthāya sambhavāmi yuge yuge.

"Whenever and wherever there is a decline in righteousness, O Arjun, and a rise in unrighteousness, at that time I manifest Myself on earth. To deliver the pious and to annihilate the miscreants, and to re-establish the principle of righteousness, I appear millennium after millennium."

Other minor gods and goddesses with separate domains like Ganesh, Kartik, Durga, Kali, Saraswati, Indra, Varuna, etc. are worshipped. In every village with a Hindu population in the Indian subcontinent, you can find many gods and goddesses settled in temples or under the trees with localized names with emotional tales associated with their glory.

Pantheism

Pantheism views the entire universe or nature itself as God or divine. It sees God as immanent, meaning that the divine is present in all things and permeates every aspect of reality. ***In pantheism, the universe and God are essentially synonymous***. Baruch Spinoza, a 17th-century Dutch philosopher, is often regarded as one of the most influential proponents of pantheism in Western philosophy. His views on pantheism are elaborated in his magnum opus, **"Ethics,"** and other writings.

Spinoza's pantheistic philosophy is characterized by the idea that the entire universe, including nature and all its elements, is a manifestation of God, or what he referred to as "Substance" or "God or Nature." ***According to Spinoza, God is not a personal, anthropomorphic being, but rather an infinite and impersonal reality that encompasses all existence.***

Spinoza's pantheism challenged conventional religious ideas of his time, leading to controversy and even accusations of atheism. His philosophy laid the groundwork for modern discussions about the relationship between nature, divinity, and human existence, and his ideas continue to inspire philosophical and theological debates to this day.

Pantheism can be found in certain interpretations of Hindu philosophy. In *Advaita Vedanta*, a non-dualistic school of thought, there is a pantheistic understanding of the Divine. According to this perspective, the ultimate reality is Brahman, an absolute, infinite, and impersonal principle. Brahman is considered the underlying essence of everything in the universe. It is immanent, meaning it permeates all existence, and transcendent, meaning it goes beyond the manifest world.

In this view, everything in the universe is an expression of Brahman, and there is no fundamental distinction between the Divine and the world. The physical world, individual souls (Atman), and the Divine are all interconnected and part of the same underlying reality. ***This pantheistic understanding emphasizes the oneness of all existence and the idea that the***

Divine is present in everything and everyone.
Adherents of this philosophy seek to realize their divine nature and achieve spiritual liberation by recognizing the unity of Brahman and the self (Atman).

Pantheism holds that God is both transcendent and immanent. It suggests that God transcends the universe but is also present within it. God is seen as encompassing and interpenetrating everything while also being more than the sum of all creation.

Here are a few examples of religious or philosophical frameworks that incorporate pantheistic elements:

Process Theology: Process theology, influenced by the works of philosophers such as Alfred North Whitehead and Charles Hartshorne, posits that God is constantly evolving and changing alongside the world. God is understood as the underlying creative force permeating all of existence while also being greater than the sum of its parts.

Sikhism: Sikhism, a religion founded in the 15th century in Punjab, India, incorporates pantheistic elements. The Sikh scripture, Guru Granth Sahib, describes God as both transcendent and immanent. God is considered formless and beyond comprehension, yet also present in all aspects of creation.

Theosophy: Theosophy, a spiritual and philosophical movement established in the late 19th century, promotes the concept of pantheism. It teaches that the divine is both immanent in the world and extends beyond it, encompassing all of creation.

Teilhardian Theology: Developed by Jesuit paleontologist and philosopher Pierre Teilhard de Chardin, Teilhardian theology suggests that God is dynamically present and actively evolving within the cosmos. God's presence is seen as permeating the world, guiding it toward a higher state of unity and consciousness.

Certain New Age and Contemporary Spiritual Beliefs: Various New Age and contemporary spiritual perspectives embrace panentheistic notions, perceiving God as an immanent and transcendent presence in the universe. *These belief systems often emphasize the interconnectedness of all things and promote personal spiritual growth and awakening.*

These examples illustrate different expressions of panentheism within religious, philosophical, and spiritual contexts, highlighting the belief in a God who is both intimately involved in the world and simultaneously transcendent.

Atheism

Atheism is the absence of belief in any God or divine beings. Atheists reject the existence of God due to the lack of empirical evidence or philosophical justifications. They typically view the natural world and human existence as products of natural processes rather than divine intervention.

Few examples of prominent individuals or organizations associated with atheism:

Richard Dawkins: Richard Dawkins is a prominent evolutionary biologist and author known for his advocacy of atheism. His book *"The God Delusion"* (2006) became a bestseller, presenting arguments against the existence of God and promoting a scientific worldview.

Christopher Hitchens: Christopher Hitchens was a renowned author, journalist, and speaker known for his staunch atheism. He wrote the book *"God Is Not Great: How Religion Poisons Everything"* (2007) in which he critiques organized religion and argues against the existence of a divine being.

American Atheists: American Atheists is an organization founded by Madalyn Murray O'Hair in 1963, advocating for the rights and representation of atheists in the United States. They actively promote secularism and work to uphold the separation of church and state.

Daniel Dennett: Daniel Dennett is a philosopher and cognitive scientist who has written extensively on consciousness, evolution, and the philosophy of mind. While not explicitly labeling himself as an atheist, his works often challenge religious beliefs and explore naturalistic explanations for phenomena.

Sam Harris: Sam Harris is a neuroscientist, philosopher, and author who is known for his critical views on religion and advocacy of atheism. His book *"The End of Faith: Religion, Terror, and the Future of Reason"* explores the dangers of religious faith and argues for a secular society based on reason and scientific inquiry.

These individuals and organizations represent different perspectives within the atheist community, actively engaging in discussions, debates, and advocacy regarding the absence of belief in deities.

Agnosticism:

"An agnostic is someone who believes that nothing is proven or unproven and that all matters remain open to question." – Bertrand Russell

Agnosticism is the belief that the existence of God or the divine is unknown, unknowable, or inherently beyond human understanding. Agnostics neither affirm nor deny the existence of God, considering it a question that is beyond the scope of human knowledge.

Agnostics often assert that insufficient evidence or lack of certainty prevents them from affirming or denying the existence of deities. Let us exploit a few examples of notable figures associated with agnosticism:

Thomas Henry Huxley: Thomas Huxley, a 19th-century English biologist and philosopher, coined the term *"agnosticism."* He believed that one should suspend judgment on religious matters due to the lack of conclusive evidence and advocated for a scientific and skeptical approach to knowledge.

Bertrand Russell: Bertrand Russell, a British philosopher, mathematician, and social critic, described himself as an agnostic. He argued that it is impossible to know whether God exists or not and advocated for a critical examination of religious claims based on reason and evidence.

Robert G. Ingersoll: Robert Ingersoll, an American lawyer and orator during the late 19th century, was known as the "Great Agnostic." He delivered numerous speeches challenging religious dogma, advocating for rational inquiry, and asserting that it is impossible to know the truth about God.

Clarence Darrow: Clarence Darrow, an American lawyer and prominent figure in the early 20th century, was known for his agnostic views. Darrow championed the separation of church and state and was a staunch advocate for scientific reasoning and skepticism.

Carl Sagan: Carl Sagan, an American astronomer, cosmologist, and science communicator, is often associated with agnosticism. While he did not explicitly identify as an agnostic, his writings and lectures frequently emphasized the importance of evidence-based reasoning and scientific inquiry while acknowledging the limitations of human knowledge.

These individuals represent notable figures who have embraced agnosticism and have contributed to discussions surrounding the limitations of human knowledge and the existence of God or ultimate reality.

Deism

"The Deist worships a God of Order, not a God of Miracles. He sees no need for divine

interventions in the clockwork universe, where natural laws reign supreme." - Voltaire

Deism holds that God exists but does not intervene in the world or human affairs after the act of creation. Deists believe that God created the universe and established natural laws but does not engage in ongoing miracles or revelation.

Deism is a philosophical belief system that posits the existence of a creator or supreme being who does not intervene in the world after its creation. Deists typically view God as a distant, impersonal entity who established natural laws governing the universe. Here is an example of deism:

Thomas Jefferson: Thomas Jefferson, one of the Founding Fathers of the United States and the principal author of the Declaration of Independence, is often associated with deism. Jefferson believed in a creator God who designed the universe but did not intervene in its affairs. He famously edited his version of the Bible, known as the **"Jefferson Bible,"** removing supernatural elements and focusing on the moral teachings of Jesus.

It's worth noting that deism as a belief system gained popularity during the Age of Enlightenment, particularly in the 17th and 18th centuries. Many Enlightenment thinkers embraced deistic principles, emphasizing reason, natural law, and the separation of religion and government. While not all Enlightenment thinkers were deists, their intellectual and philosophical contributions influenced the development of deistic thought.

It's important to note that these categories are not exhaustive, and beliefs about God can be highly diverse and nuanced even within specific religious or philosophical traditions. The interpretation of God can vary greatly, encompassing personal experiences, cultural influences, and philosophical reflections.

Existence of God in the Eyes of Science

God is often considered a supernatural, matter of faith and belief that transcends the physical world. Science is the study of the natural world, and it uses the scientific method to test hypotheses and develop theories. The scientific method involves making observations, forming hypotheses, testing hypotheses, and drawing conclusions. Science has been very successful in explaining the natural world, but it has not been able to prove or disprove the existence of God. This is because the existence of God is a question of faith, and faith is not something that can be tested using the scientific method. Some people believe that the complexity and order of the universe are evidence of a creator. Others believe that the universe can be explained by natural processes without the need for a creator.

The question of God's existence has been debated for centuries, and there are various arguments put forward by both believers and skeptics. Some of the commonly discussed arguments for the existence of God include:

1. Cosmological Argument: This argument suggests that the universe must have had a cause or a *"first mover"* that initiated its existence. Theists posit that this uncaused cause is God. However, critics of this argument propose alternative explanations, such as the multiverse hypothesis or the possibility of an eternal universe. Despite these criticisms, the cosmological argument remains a popular argument for the existence of God. It is a simple and straightforward argument that is easy to understand. It is also an argument that has been endorsed by many famous philosophers and theologians, including Aristotle, Thomas Aquinas, and Gottfried Wilhelm Leibniz.

2. Teleological Argument (Argument from Design): This argument asserts that the complexity and order observed in the natural world imply the existence of an intelligent designer, which believers identify as God. Critics counter this by proposing natural selection and the laws of physics as sufficient explanations for the apparent design.

3. Moral Argument: This argument contends that the existence of objective moral values and duties necessitates the existence of a moral lawgiver, often conceived of as God. Conversely, some atheists argue that moral values can be explained through social evolution and empathy.

4. Ontological Argument: This is a more abstract argument that seeks to prove God's existence based on the concept of a *"perfect being."* Critics often find issues with the logic of this argument.

5. The Big Bang theory is the prevailing cosmological model for the observable universe from the earliest known periods through its subsequent large-scale evolution. The model accounts for the fact that the universe expanded from a very high density and high-temperature state, and offers a comprehensive explanation for a broad range of phenomena. It includes the abundance of light elements, the cosmic microwave background, large-scale structure, and Hubble's law. Some people believe that the Big Bang theory is evidence of a creator, while others believe that it can be explained by natural processes without the need for a creator.

6. The theory of evolution is a scientific theory that accounts for the diversity of life on Earth. The theory states that all living organisms are descended from common ancestors and that the diversity of life is due to natural selection. Some people believe that the theory of evolution is evidence against the existence of God, while others believe that it is compatible with their religious beliefs.

The study of consciousness is a complex and challenging field of research. Scientists are still trying to understand what consciousness is and how it arises. Some people believe that consciousness is evidence of a soul, while others believe that it can be explained by natural processes

It's important to recognize that none of these arguments provides definitive scientific proof of God's existence. They are philosophical and metaphysical arguments that aim to make a case for God's existence based on logic and reason. However, they are not empirical evidence that can be tested and verified scientifically.

Belief in God is deeply personal and often rooted in faith, spirituality, and personal experiences rather than **scientific evidence**. Individuals may find spiritual fulfillment and purpose through their belief in a higher power, ***but these experiences are subjective and not subject to scientific verification.***

Science and spirituality can coexist for many people, as they address different aspects of human understanding and exploration. Many scientists find no conflict between their scientific work and their personal beliefs in God or spirituality. The great scientist Albert Einstein says- ***"The more I study science, the more I believe in God."***

These are the perspectives of individual scientists and should not be seen as representative of the entire scientific community. Views on the existence of God are personal and can vary greatly among scientists, just as they do in the broader population.

However, it's essential to respect and understand that the realm of science and the realm of faith are distinct and serve different purposes in the human quest for knowledge and meaning.

Understanding the Nature of God

Understanding the nature of God is a complex and profound concept that has been contemplated and debated throughout human history. Different religious, philosophical, and spiritual traditions offer diverse perspectives on the nature of God. Here are some common aspects and interpretations that can contribute to understanding the nature of God:

Transcendence and Immanence:

Many belief systems describe *God as both transcendent and immanent.* Transcendence refers to God being beyond the physical world and human comprehension, existing in a realm beyond human perception. Immanence refers to God's presence within and throughout creation, intimately connected to the world and all living beings. In the Bhagavad Gita, Lord Krishna emphasizes His omnipresence and how He pervades everything in the universe. Here is a quote from Chapter 9, Verse 4, where Lord Krishna describes His all-pervading nature:

मया ततमिदं सर्वं जगदव्यक्तमूर्तिना।
मत्स्थानि सर्वभूतानि न चाहं तेष्ववस्थितः॥ **गीता ॥ 9.4 ॥**

mayā tatamidaṁ sarvaṁ jagadavyaktamūrtinā
matsthāni sarvabhūtāni na cāhaṁ teshvavasthitaḥ

In this verse, Lord Krishna proclaims that the entire universe, both manifested and unmanifested, is pervaded by Him. He is present everywhere as the unmanifested essence that sustains and permeates all living beings and the entire creation. However, even though He is present in all things, He remains transcendental and not limited by material manifestations.

Hebrew Bible says though transcendent, the Creator God is not distant from his creation. He remains actively involved, providing for its needs, guiding its course, and intervening in human history. (Psalm 103:19, Proverbs 16:9)

The above references highlight the omnipresence and immanence of the Divine, emphasizing that God's presence extends beyond the material world and transcends its limitations.

Attributes:

Various qualities and attributes are ascribed to God across different traditions. These attributes may include omnipotence (all-powerful), omniscience (all-knowing), omnipresence (present everywhere), eternal, loving (**"God is love."-Bible, 1 John 4:8),** Just, merciful, giver, and compassionate. Different religious and philosophical traditions emphasize specific attributes based on their teachings, scriptures, and God realization.

Creator:

God is often seen as the ***creator of the universe*** and all that exists within it. The concept of creation varies, ranging from a literal interpretation of a divine act of bringing the universe into existence to more metaphorical interpretations. It emphasizes God as the underlying force or intelligence behind the universe's existence. As God is the creator, He is present everywhere, as Lord Krishna declared in Gita.

अहमात्मा गुडाकेश सर्वभूताशयस्थितः।
अहमादिश्च मध्यं च भूतानामन्त एव च॥ गीता ॥ 10.20॥

"Aham ātmā guḍākeśa sarvabhūtāśayasthitaḥ
Aham ādiścha madhyaṁ cha bhūtānāmanta eva cha.

This means Krishna is the essence of the universe and is present within all living beings. He is the cause of creation, existence, and destruction of the creations, the entire universe.

The Bible portrays creation not as an accident or whim, but as a purposeful act aimed at establishing a good and flourishing life. *God sees his creation as "very good" (Genesis 1:31) and entrusts humanity with the responsibility to "tend and keep" it (Genesis 2:15).*

Overall, God is the creator and omnipresent as the divine essence dwelling within all living beings. He asserts his role as the source, sustainer, and ultimate reality underlying the entire creation.

Personal and Impersonal Aspects:

Some belief systems view God as a personal being with whom one can have a personal relationship. This perspective often includes ideas of prayer, communication, and guidance from God. Many sages, monks, sad gurus, bhaktas, and saints have direct communications with gods and goddesses. They have seen the god and talked with Him. For example, Saint Ramakrishna Paramhamsa, (the guru of Swami

Vivekananda), Swami Vivekananda had direct communications with the *goddess Dakhineswar Kali.* Eknath, a revered 16th-century Hindu saint, poet, and philosopher, gained fame as the author of the Eknathi Bhagavata, composed in the Marathi language. He was a devoted follower of Vitthal, the Hindu deity embodying Krishna. Legend has it that Vitthal, in the guise of a servant, selflessly served Saint Eknath for many years without the saint's awareness. When the truth eventually came to light, Vitthal mysteriously disappeared. This tale beautifully illustrates the profound and mysterious bond between a devotee and their divine deity. On the other hand, some traditions perceive God as an impersonal force or principle, transcending personal characteristics and individual relationships.

Unity and Oneness:

Many belief systems emphasize the unity and oneness of God. They suggest that God is the ultimate source and essence of all that exists, and everything is interconnected within this divine unity. This perspective often aligns with the idea that all manifestations of existence are expressions of the same divine reality. Without Him, we can't imagine any creation. Nature, stars, galaxies, black holes, comets, white holes, the oceans, the beasts, living and non-living, and everything that is seen or unseen is the manifestation of one supreme power God.

The Bible emphatically rejects the existence of other gods besides the one true God, Yahweh (Hebrew name of god). Deuteronomy 6:4 states, ***"Hear, O Israel:***

The Lord your God is one Lord." This principle is reaffirmed throughout the Old Testament. Similarly, New Testament passages like John 17:3 and Romans 3:29 reiterate the uniqueness and oneness of God.

Lord Krishna said in the Gita;

मयाध्यक्षेण प्रकृतिः सूयते सचराचरम्।
हेतुनानेन कौन्तेय जगद्‌द्वीपरिवर्तते॥ गीता ॥9.10 ॥

Mayādhyakṣeṇa prakṛtiḥ sūyate sacarācaram
Hetunānena kaunteya jagadbhīparivartate.

"Under my instructions and supervision the Prakriti (nature) gives birth to the living and non-living beings in the universe. This is the reason why the cosmos revolves and continues its action.

Mystery and Ineffability:

The nature of God is often described as mysterious and beyond complete human comprehension. Many traditions acknowledge the limitations of human understanding when it comes to grasping the full nature of God. The concept of God's ineffability recognizes that words and concepts fall short of capturing the **entirety** of the divine reality.

The Bible says- *"No one has ever seen God at any time. But the one and only Son, who is near the father's heart, has declared him."* - John 1:18

This verse describes the paradox of God's nature: He is invisible and unknowable through direct perception, yet He reveals Himself through His Son, Jesus Christ.

Similarly, the conversation of the mythical hero Arjun with Lord Krishna reveals the mysterious and undescribed nature of the Godhead. He is the only one who knows himself none of the others.

स्वयमेवात्मनात्मानं वेत्थ त्वं पुरुषोत्तम।

भूतभावन भूतेश देवदेव जगत्पते॥ गीता   ॥ 10.15 ॥

Swayam evātmanātmānam vettvam tvam puruṣottama.
Bhūta-bhāvana bhūteśa devadeva jagatpate.Gita

"O Supreme Person, by realizing Yourself as the Self through Yourself, O best among men, and by Your power, You pervade and support all beings as the Supreme Lord, the God of gods, the Lord of the universe."

Emancipator and Savior:

God is the emancipator and protector of all devotees and all His creation. As God is a compassionate, and loving one He forgives everyone who comes and completely surrenders before Him. In the Bhagavad Gita, Lord Krishna, the Supreme Personality of Godhead, speaks to Arjun and imparts spiritual wisdom and guidance. In chapter 18, Verse 66 of the Bhagavad Gita Lord Krishna says:

सर्वधर्मान्परित्यज्य मामेकं शरणं व्रज ।

अहं त्वा सर्वपापेभ्यो मोक्षयिष्यामि मा शुचः ॥ गीता ॥ 18.66 ॥

sarva-dharmān parityajya māmekam śaraṇam vraja
aham tvām sarva-pāpebhyo mokṣayiṣyāmi mā śucaḥ

In this verse, Lord Krishna is urging Arjun to let go of all other temporary or materialistic paths and surrender himself completely to the Supreme. He assures Arjun that by doing so, he will be freed from all sins and **attain liberation or emancipation (moksha)**. Another verse is from Chapter 18, Verse 58 where Lord Krishna says;

मच्चित्तः सर्वदुर्गाणि मत्प्रसादात्तरिष्यसि ।

अथ चेत्त्वमहङ्कारान्न श्रोष्यसि विनङ्क्ष्यसि ॥

mac-cittaḥ sarva-durgāṇi mat-prasādāttariṣyasi
atha cet tvam ahaṅkārān na śroṣyasi vinaṅkṣyasi

In this verse, Lord Krishna assures that those who keep their minds and consciousness fixed on Him, surrender to Him with devotion, and follow His guidance, He will protect them from all difficulties and challenges. **The key is to have complete faith and surrender to the will of the Supreme**. Let the devotees surrender before Him with the prayer-

"शरणागत मांग जगदीश रक्ष"

"I surrender myself before your lotus feet, safeguard me the Divine Lord."

This phrase is often used as a prayer or mantra seeking protection and refuge from the Supreme Lord, Jagadish (the Lord of the Universe), by expressing one's surrender and devotion.

The Bible contains several verses and teachings that emphasize the idea of surrendering oneself to God and putting trust in Him. Here are some verses that highlight the theme of surrender in the Bible:

1. Proverbs 3:5-6 (New International Version):
"Trust in the Lord with all your heart and lean not on your understanding; in all your ways submit to him, and he will make your paths straight."

2. Matthew 16:24 (New Testament, Jesus' teaching):
"Then Jesus said to his disciples, 'Whoever wants to be my disciple must deny themselves and take up their cross and follow me."

3. James 4:7-8a (New Testament):
"Submit yourselves, then, to God. Resist the devil, and he will flee from you. Come near to God, and he will come near to you."

Isaiah 43:3-4:

"For I am the Lord your God, the Holy One of Israel, your Savior. I gave Egypt as your ransom, Cush and Seba as your exchange. Because you were precious in my sight and

honored, and I loved you, therefore I gave men in your exchange, and peoples in your stead."

These verses and teachings encourage individuals to surrender their will and concerns to God, trusting in His wisdom and guidance. The act of surrendering is seen as an act of faith and humility, acknowledging God's sovereignty and seeking His help in navigating life's challenges. Surrendering to God is believed to bring peace, protection, and spiritual growth in the Christian tradition.

Multiple Manifestations:

Some traditions propose that God can manifest in different forms or aspects to facilitate human understanding and connection. These manifestations, such as avatars, messengers, prophets, gurus etc.

Multiple Manifestations or divine incarnations, are seen as expressions of the divine in ways that are accessible and relatable to humanity.

Hinduism:

In Hinduism Lord Vishnu is believed to have taken several avatars (incarnations) to restore cosmic order and protect righteousness. The ten most prominent avatars are *Matsya* **(fish),** *Kurma* **(tortoise),** *Varaha* **(boar),** *Narasimha* **(half-lion, half-human),** *Vamana* **(dwarf),** *Parashurama* **(warrior sage),** *Rama* **(Prince of Ayodhya),** *Balarama* **(Krishna's elder brother),** *Buddha,* **and** *Kalki* (yet to come). Lord Shiva, the destroyer and transformer, takes various forms representing different aspects. Some notable forms include *Nataraja* **(Lord of Dance)**, *Ardhanarishvara* **(half-male, half-female)**, **and** *Dakshinamurti* **(the silent teacher)**.

Goddess Durga is known for her fierce form and protective nature. She has different manifestations such as ***Kali*** (the fierce form of the goddess**),** ***Parvati*** (the gentle and nurturing aspect of the mother goddess), and ***Chamunda*** (the slayer of demons). Likely the concept of the Divine Mother is prevalent in Hinduism. She is known by various names like Devi, Shakti, or Mahadevi. Some well-known forms of the Divine Mother include ***Lakshmi*** (goddess of wealth and prosperity), ***Saraswati*** (goddess of knowledge and arts), and ***Kali*** (goddess of time and destruction). These are just a few examples of the many manifestations of God in Hinduism. Each form or incarnation carries a specific purpose and symbolism in the cosmic order.

Gurus, Prophets, or Messengers:

You may also find Gurus, prophets, or messengers in various religions, here are a few examples from different faith traditions:

Prophet Muhammad (Islam): Prophet Muhammad is considered the final prophet of Islam and the messenger of Allah (God). Muslims believe that he received revelations from Allah, which were compiled into the holy book, ***the Quran.***

Jesus Christ (Christianity): Christians believe that Jesus Christ is the Son of God and the Messiah who came to save humanity. He is regarded as both a prophet and the central figure of Christianity.

Moses (Judaism): Moses is an important prophet in Judaism who received the Ten Commandments from God on Mount Sinai. He is considered a great leader and the liberator of the Israelites from slavery in Egypt.

Guru Nanak Dev Ji (Sikhism): Guru Nanak Dev Ji is the founder of Sikhism and is considered the first of the ten Sikh Gurus. He taught the principles of equality, justice, and devotion to God.

Zoroaster (Zoroastrianism): Zoroaster, also known as Zarathustra, is the founder of Zoroastrianism. He is considered a prophet and revealed the teachings and scriptures of the Zoroastrian faith.

These are just a few examples, and many more prophets and messengers in different religious traditions are believed to have been chosen by a higher power to convey divine messages and guide their respective communities.

It's essential to recognize that different individuals and cultures may have diverse interpretations of the nature of God. These interpretations often arise from a combination of scriptural teachings, personal experiences, philosophical reflections, and cultural influences. *The nature of God remains a deeply contemplative and subjective topic that*

The Role of Faith and Spirituality

Faith and spirituality play significant roles in the lives of individuals and communities, offering a framework for meaning, purpose, and connection with the divine or transcendent aspects of existence. Faith and spirituality may influence the lives of humans in many ways.

Faith and spirituality provide a sense of meaning and purpose in life. They address existential questions about the nature of reality, the purpose of human existence, and the significance of our actions and relationships. Through faith and spirituality, individuals find a larger context for their lives and a sense of belonging to something greater than themselves. They facilitate a connection with the divine. However, it is understood within a particular belief system. ***They provide a means to experience and relate to a higher power, God, or the ultimate reality. This connection fosters a sense of reverence, awe, and devotion, allowing individuals to deepen their relationship with the divine and seek guidance, blessings, solace, and inspiration***.

Faith and spirituality often provide a moral and ethical framework for us humans. They offer guiding principles and values that shape an individual's behavior and decision-making. Many religious and spiritual traditions emphasize virtues such as compassion, kindness, honesty, and justice, which help individuals navigate ethical dilemmas and cultivate a sense of responsibility toward others and the world.

Faith and spirituality support inner transformation and personal growth through spiritual practices such as prayer, meditation, self-reflection, and ritual. These practices can lead to increased self-acceptance, emotional well-being, and the development of virtues and qualities that align with the spiritual path. They also foster a sense of community and social support. Including a shared belief system and a gathering place for individuals to come together, worship, celebrate, and support one another. Religious and spiritual communities often offer a sense of belonging, social connections, and a support network in times of joy and adversity.

Faith and spirituality offer resources for coping with life's challenges and adversities. They provide solace, hope, and comfort during difficult times, helping individuals find meaning, strength, and resilience in the face of adversity. They can provide a sense of perspective, acceptance, and trust in a higher power or divine plan.

Faith and spirituality facilitate transcendence beyond the ordinary, mundane aspects of life. They open individuals to expanded states of consciousness, allowing them to glimpse a greater reality beyond the physical realm. This expanded consciousness brings a sense of awe, wonder, and connection to the mysteries of existence.

It's important to note that faith and spirituality are deeply personal and subject to personal experiences. They can be expressed and practiced within organized religious traditions or through individual spiritual paths. The role of faith and spirituality can vary from person to person, depending on their beliefs, cultural background, and personal journey of seeking meaning and connection.

Chapter Three

The Importance of Self-Awareness

The Relationship between Self-awareness and God Consciousness

The relationship between self-awareness and God consciousness is a profound and interdependent one. Let us have an exploration of how self-awareness and God-consciousness are connected:

What is the Self?

"Who am I? That is the fundamental question. If you find the answer to that, you will find the answer to everything else."- Ramana Maharshi

Is the self a physical body or anything more? Is the self a body made of five gross elements or beyond that? According to Eastern philosophies, such as the Indian spiritual doctrine and scriptures, the self is identified as the pure soul, known as Atman. In this perspective, the self is considered immortal, emphasizing a profound and enduring essence that goes beyond the material aspects of the physical body. Upanishad says

"Ayam ātmā brahma." (Mandukya Upanishad, 1.2) "This self (Atman) is Brahman." The self is Atman, and it is immortal. The Gita also affirms this truth.

नैनं छिन्दन्ति शस्त्राणि नैनं दहति पावकः।
न चैनं क्लेदयन्त्यापो न शोषयति मारुतः॥ गीता ॥ 2.23॥

Nainaṁ chindanti śastrāṇi nainaṁ dahati pāvakah
Na cainaṁ kledayantyāpo na śoṣayati mārutah.

In this verse, Lord Krishna explains the eternal nature of the soul (Atman). According to Godhead, the soul is indestructible and unaffected by physical elements or external forces. Weapons cannot harm it, fire cannot burn it, water cannot wet it, and wind cannot dry it.

The verse emphasizes the immortal and unchanging nature of the soul, highlighting its transcendence over the perishable body and material existence.

However, the so-called most intelligent man in the universe most of the time can't understand his true nature, his true self due to different factors leading to illusions. Understanding the self is very important to understanding God consciousness.

Self-awareness as a Path to God Consciousness:

Self-awareness is a crucial aspect of the journey toward God consciousness. By cultivating self-awareness, individuals gain insight into their thoughts, emotions, beliefs, and behaviors. *This introspective process helps individuals identify and transcend ego-driven patterns, attachments, and illusions that hinder their connection with the divine.* Self-awareness allows individuals to recognize and align with their true nature, which is often described as the divine spark within.

Dissolution of the Illusory Self:

Self-awareness can lead to the dissolution of the illusory self, the ego, which is characterized by a sense of separateness, identification with the physical body, and attachment to personal desires and outcomes. As self-awareness deepens, individuals realize that their true essence is not confined to the limited boundaries of the ego but is connected to the larger fabric of existence. This dissolution of the illusory self creates space for the emergence of God consciousness.

Self-awareness opens the inner eyes of the self and he realizes that *"Tat tvam asi."* (Chandogya Upanishad, 6.8.7**)** means **"That thou art."** It expresses the unity of the individual soul (Atman) and the universal soul (Brahman).

Recognizing the Divine Within:

Self-awareness enables individuals to recognize the divine presence within themselves. By becoming aware of their thoughts, emotions, and inner experiences, individuals may realize that there is a deeper consciousness or essence beyond the surface level of their identity. This recognition of the divine essence within oneself is a significant step toward experiencing God consciousness.

Interconnectedness and Unity:

Self-awareness also reveals the interconnectedness and unity of all existence. As individuals deepen their self-awareness, they start to perceive the interdependence between themselves and the world around them. A great saint Raman Maharshi says-***"You are having continuous vision of God. Instead of seeing X, Y, Z, why don't you see God in everyone/everything."***
Similarly, the Bible says(Galatians 3:28☺) "There is neither Jew nor Gentile, neither slave nor free, nor is there male and female, for you are all one in Christ Jesus." This verse transcends societal divisions, highlighting the shared humanity and potential for unity in Christ. This is the recognition of interconnectedness aligns with the understanding of God consciousness, which emphasizes the underlying unity of all beings and the interconnectedness of the divine within each individual.

Expanded Consciousness and Divine Revelation:

Self-awareness can lead to expanded consciousness, allowing individuals to transcend limited perspectives and access higher levels of awareness. In this expanded state of consciousness, individuals may experience divine revelations, insights, and wisdom that go beyond the ordinary intellect. This expanded awareness provides glimpses into the nature of God consciousness and deepens the connection with the divine.

Integration of Self and God:

As self-awareness deepens and individuals cultivate God consciousness, there is an integration of the self and the divine. The boundaries between the personal self and the transcendent aspect of existence become more permeable, and individuals experience a sense of oneness and unity with the divine. This integration allows individuals to live in alignment with their true nature and express the qualities of love, compassion, and wisdom associated with God-consciousness. The self-realized one declares; ***"Aham brahmāsmi."*** (Brihadaranyaka Upanishad, 1.4.10). ***"I am Brahman."*** There is unity of self and Brahman. The soul is not separated from the supreme soul or Brahman.

It's important to note that self-awareness and the realization of God consciousness are **iterative processes** that unfold over time. They are influenced by various factors, including spiritual practices, contemplation, personal experiences, ***and guidance from Gurus' spiritual traditions.*** The journey toward God consciousness often involves a deepening of self-awareness and a simultaneous expansion of one's connection with the divine.

Tools for Developing Self-awareness

Developing self-awareness is a lifelong journey that involves conscious effort and practice. Fortunately, various tools and techniques can aid in the development of self-awareness. Self-awareness can drive you safely toward the understanding of spiritual ethics and god realization. Here are some effective tools for cultivating self-awareness:

Mindfulness Meditation

Mindfulness meditation involves focusing your attention on the present moment and observing your thoughts, emotions, and bodily sensations without judgment about God and belief systems. It aims to increase self-awareness, reduce stress, and provide mental clarity and emotional well-being. Remember, the objective of mindful meditation is not to suppress thoughts or emotions but to observe them with curiosity and a non-judgmental approach. Regular practice of mindfulness meditation can enhance self-awareness by helping you become more attuned to your inner experiences and thought patterns about God consciousness.

Journaling

Writing in a journal can be a powerful tool for self-reflection and self-discovery. By putting your thoughts and feelings on paper, you gain clarity and insight into your experiences, beliefs, and values about spirituality.

Journaling can help identify patterns, feelings, and triggers, about god. Remember, there is no right or wrong way to journaling. You can write in structure form whatever thought caught your mind on god and His actions. Let them come out fluently without judgment. Observe what thought pattern about divine senses is shaping your objectives. Make it a regular habit to get the true divine self in you. Journaling is definitely a great pathway toward God consciousness nothing to doubt about it.

Self-Reflection and Self-Questioning

Setting aside dedicated time for self-reflection allows you to examine your thoughts, emotions, and behaviors. Ask yourself open-ended questions such as ***"What am I feeling right now?" or "Why did I react that way?"*** This process encourages introspection deepens self-awareness and leads you to attend God consciousness on due process.

Feedback from Others

Seeking and being open to feedback from trusted spiritual individuals in your life can provide valuable insights into your blind spots and areas for improvement. Others may offer perspectives that you haven't considered, helping you gain a more accurate understanding of yourself. ***However, your inner strength and inner child can be the real pathfinder. No external validation is required for subjective enlightenment in the spiritual arena.***

Emotional Awareness

Developing emotional awareness involves recognizing and understanding your own emotions. Pay attention to your emotional experiences about the divine throughout the day, labeling and acknowledging your emotions without judgment. When your emotion is triggered and directed toward the spiritual end, then it is a good sign of personal growth. This practice helps you develop a greater understanding of your emotional patterns and triggers.

Awareness of the Physical body

Cultivating the awareness of your physical body involves tuning into your physical sensations and cues to a religious gathering or discourse. Pay attention to how your body feels in different situations, noticing areas of tension, relaxation, or discomfort. This awareness can provide valuable information about your emotional state and help you understand how your body responds to various stimuli. Remember body is a temple where God lives. Body clarifies the truth to yourself. It is the body by which you can connect to God and realize God consciousness.

Retreats and Silent Reflection

Participating in retreats or engaging in periods of silent reflection allows you to disconnect from external distractions and focus inward. These dedicated periods of solitude and silence provide an opportunity for deep self-exploration and heightened self-awareness.

Remember that developing self-awareness is an ongoing practice that requires patience, commitment, and self-compassion. Combining multiple tools and techniques that resonate with you can create a well-rounded approach to self-awareness development.

Overcoming Obstacles to Self-awareness

Overcoming obstacles to self-awareness can be challenging, but with persistence and intention, it is possible to navigate through them. You can encounter some common obstacles to self-awareness and strategies for overcoming them:

Denial and Resistance:

Denial and resistance can prevent us from acknowledging and accepting some aspects of ourselves that may be uncomfortable or challenging. To overcome this obstacle, it's essential to cultivate a willingness to face the truth about ourselves and our experiences. Practice self-compassion and create a safe and non-judgmental space to explore and accept all aspects of who you are. In the area of God consciousness, such types of obstacles may be manifold.

Fear of Vulnerability:

"It is what we hide that becomes what hunts us." - Carl Jung

The fear of being vulnerable and exposing our true selves can hinder self-awareness. Recognize that everyone is prone to vulnerability and you make it your strength and an opportunity for growth. Engage in honest and open self-reflection in a routine manner. Step out of your comfort zone to share your thoughts, feelings, and experiences with a spiritual angle with trusted individuals and spiritual teachers who can provide support and understanding.

Distractions and Busyness:

Our modern lifestyles are often filled with distractions, busyness, and constant stimulation. These external influences can prevent us from turning inward and engaging in self-reflection. Prioritize moments of solitude and quiet. Fix specific time for self-reflection, and minimize outer world distractions. Every step be taken to avoid electronic devices to create space for self-awareness.

Lack of Mindfulness:

Mindfulness, the practice of being fully present in the moment, is crucial for developing self-awareness. If you find yourself constantly preoccupied with thoughts of the past or future, it can be challenging to cultivate self-awareness. Incorporate mindfulness techniques, such as deep breathing exercises or body scans, into your daily routine to bring yourself into the present moment and cultivate self-awareness. When you are pursuing God consciousness, mindfulness is indeed necessary.

Defensive Mechanisms:

We all have defense mechanisms, such as denial, rationalization, or projection that protect us from uncomfortable emotions or truths. Becoming aware of these defense mechanisms is the first step in overcoming them. Practice self-compassion and cultivate a non-judgmental attitude toward yourself. Engage in self-reflection to uncover the underlying emotions and beliefs that may be driving these defense mechanisms.

External Validation and Comparison:

Expecting external validation and constantly comparing ourselves to others can distort our self-perception and hinder self-awareness. Focus on developing an internal locus of control, where you rely on your values, strengths, objectives, and goals rather than seeking approval from others. *Practice self-acceptance and embrace your unique journey and qualities. Never underestimate yourself. Remember you are a unique creation of the god and you have every scope to know Him.* It's your own business, so why long for external validation? Thich Nhat Hanh rightly says-***"There is nothing to be attained. This is the ultimate freedom. Nothing to achieve, nothing to become. There is only here, only now."***

Emotional Avoidance:

Avoiding or suppressing emotions can create a barrier to self-awareness. Allow yourself to experience and explore a wide range of emotions without judgment.

Develop emotional resilience and practice healthy emotional expression through techniques like journaling. Direct your emotion toward God, your creator. Make it your habit. You may talk to a trusted friend, or engage in creative writing.

Limited Perspectives:

Holding rigid beliefs or being stuck in a narrow mindset can limit your self-awareness. Cultivate a growth mindset that embraces learning, openness, and curiosity. Seek out diverse perspectives, engage in dialogue with others who hold different views, and be open to challenging your own beliefs and assumptions. If you have a fixed mindset, you have to convert it into a growth mindset. A growth mindset can enrich you with the spiritual emotion you have to find the proper way to God consciousness.

Overcoming obstacles to self-awareness requires patience, persistence, and self-compassion. Embrace the journey of self-discovery, and remember that it is a lifelong process. By actively working through these obstacles, you can gradually enhance your self-awareness and develop a deeper understanding of yourself. Once you understand yourself then you can explore more for the longing for spiritual awareness.

Chapter Four

Practices for Cultivating God Consciousness

Meditation

Meditation is a practice that involves training the mind to focus and redirect thoughts. It is a technique that has been practiced for thousands of years and is found in various religious and spiritual traditions, as well as secular contexts. It is definitely an answer to our monkey mind game.

"The mind is like a monkey jumping from branch to branch. If you try to force it to stop, it will only become more agitated. Instead, simply watch the monkey mind with curiosity and detachment. Eventually, it will get tired and come to rest." - Swami Vivekananda

Meditation offers numerous benefits for mental, emotional, and physical well-being

Basic Principles:

Meditation typically involves finding a quiet and comfortable space where you can sit or lie down in a relaxed posture. The practice revolves around cultivating a state of focused attention and awareness. The primary objective is to bring your attention to the present moment and observe your thoughts, emotions, and bodily sensations without judgment or attachment.

Types of Meditation:

There are several types of meditation, each with its own focus and technique. Some common forms include:

- **Mindfulness Meditation**: Mindfulness meditation involves directing your attention to the present moment and observing your thoughts, feelings, and bodily sensations as they arise without judgment. It cultivates a sense of non-reactivity and acceptance.

- **Loving-Kindness Meditation**: Loving-kindness meditation involves directing feelings of compassion, love, and goodwill toward oneself, loved ones, neutral individuals, and even difficult individuals. It aims to develop empathy, kindness, and a sense of connectedness with others.

- **Transcendental Meditation**: Transcendental meditation involves the use of a specific mantra or sound to focus the mind and achieve a state of deep relaxation and inner peace. It is often practiced for shorter periods and is known for its simplicity and accessibility. In spiritual guidance, such a type of meditation is essential for understanding of God.

- **Visualization Meditation:** Visualization meditation involves creating mental images or visualizing positive experiences, places, or goals. It harnesses the power of the mind's imagination to evoke relaxation, inspiration, or healing.

- **Chakra meditation:** Chakra meditation is a type of meditation that focuses on the chakras, (seven) which are energy centers in the body. It is said to help balance the chakras and promote physical and emotional well-being. It can be done with proper guidance from an expert. It can help in spiritual understanding.

- **Yoga meditation:** Yoga meditation is a type of meditation that is practiced in conjunction with yoga postures. It is said to help deepen the connection between the mind, body, and soul.

Benefits of Meditation:

Regular meditation practice can have a profound impact on mental, emotional, and physical well-being. Some of the benefits include:

- *Stress Reduction:* Meditation helps to calm the mind, relax the body, and reduce stress by activating the body's relaxation response.
- *Improved Focus and Concentration:* The trained mind stays present and focused. Meditation enhances attention span, concentration, and cognitive abilities.
- *Emotional Well-being:* Meditation promotes emotional regulation, resilience, and the ability to respond to challenging situations with greater clarity and calmness. It can **reduce symptoms of anxiety, depression, and emotional distress**.

- *Increased Self-Awareness:* Meditation cultivates self-awareness by helping individuals observe their thoughts, emotions, and patterns of behavior without judgment. It allows for greater understanding and insight into one's inner experiences
- *Enhanced Physical Health:* Some studies suggest that meditation can have positive effects on physical health, including lowered blood pressure, improved immune function, and better sleep quality.
- *Emotional connection with a supernatural power:* Meditation increases the concentration in the mind and increases the farsightedness in the man practicing. The Chakra meditation activates the seven chakras giving different specific results and connecting with a supernatural power God.

Starting a Meditation Practice:

To start a meditation practice, consider the following tips:

- Begin with short sessions: Start with just a few minutes of meditation and gradually increase the duration as you become more comfortable.
- Find a comfortable posture: Sit or lie down in a position that is comfortable for you. It can be cross-legged on a cushion, sitting on a chair, or lying down.
- Choose a quiet space: Find a quiet environment where you can minimize distractions and interruptions.

- Set a timer: Use a timer to set a specific duration for your meditation session, so you can remain focused without worrying about the time.

- Focus on your breath or a chosen object: Direct your attention to your breath, noticing the sensation of the breath entering and leaving your body. Alternatively, you can choose a specific object of focus, such as a mantra, an object (lotus feet of your guru, God), or a candle flame.

- Be patient and non-judgmental: Be patient with yourself and your practice. It's natural for the mind to wander during meditation. But regular practice can calm down your mind and be focussed on a particular deity, object, or image where you wish to be.

Prayer

"Prayer is the most powerful form of energy one can generate; it is a force as real as terrestrial gravity. Prayer, like radium, is a source of luminous, self-generating energy.... In prayer, human beings seek to augment their finite energy by addressing themselves to the infinite source of all energy. When we pray, we link ourselves with the inexhaustible motive power that spins the universe. We pray a part of this power be apportioned, to our needs. Even in asking, our human deficiencies are filled, and we arise strengthened.... When we address God in fervent prayer, we change both soul and body for better."-Dr Alexis Carrel

It is a very clear concept of prayer. Prayer is a way to transfer energy from the god to the devotee and a force of belief. It is often associated with faith and a strong belief system. It is an offering of heart to a beloved deity or the all-mighty with form or without form. Nobody can measure the intensity and emotion involved in a prayer. Prayer gives relaxation, the heart fills with compassion and love. Further, it is a form of surrender before a personal god. Prayer is a practice that involves communicating with a higher power or divine entity. It is a deeply personal affair. Prayer has been accepted in spiritual practice across various religious traditions and belief systems. Prayer serves as a means of expressing gratitude, offering devotion, seeking guidance, offering supplications, and fostering a connection with the divine.

A prayer is a form of communication with a higher power, whether it is God, the Universe, a deity, or a personal concept of the divine. It involves expressing thoughts, emotions, desires, and intentions to this higher power. Prayer can be spoken aloud, silently, or written down. Prayer can be a personal practice, where individuals engage in private conversations with the divine. It can also be a communal practice, where people come together to pray collectively, such as in religious services, gatherings, or rituals.

Example of a prayer;

हमें इतनी शक्ति देना दाता, मन का विश्वास कमजोर हो ना।

हम चाहें विजय देखें, कभी हारे ना हारे।

दूर गगन में खड़े, एक जगमगाहट बारिश की हो,

पूरी श्रद्धा यहां मन से, यह आवाज आएगी हमारी।

"Grant us such strength, O Creator,

That our belief in ourselves never weakens.

May we witness the victory,

Never experiencing defeat?

Standing beneath the distant sky,

Amidst the resounding rain,

With complete devotion in our hearts,

Our voices will be heard."

This is a secular prayer adopted in India and school children get inspiration from the prayer practiced in schools.

Types of Prayer:

Different types of prayer serve various purposes:

Adoration and Gratitude: In such types of prayer the devotees express their gratitude toward the divine god. The expression of love, reverence, and loyalty toward the divine for His blessings, guidance, and presence in one's life. This is a form of the obligation of the devotees to the divine to fulfill their needs, showing the proper direction in the journey to the destination. The relationship between Bhakta/devotee and Bhagban/Divine is based on selfless love. However, bhaktas get everything without asking for it, for which the devotees offer the gratitude prayer.

Petition and Supplication: Petitionary prayer involves making requests or seeking help from the divine. Because the divine is present everywhere and kind to his devotees. He gives everything to the petitioner if approached properly. Such a type of prayer can include asking for guidance, healing, protection, or support for oneself or others.

Intercessory Prayer: Intercessory prayer is the act of praying to the divine on behalf of others. The gist of the prayer may include asking the divine to provide aid, healing, or blessings for individuals or specific situations. It is a powerful way to show love and compassion for those in need, and it can have a profound impact on their lives.

The Bible is full of examples of intercessory prayer. Jesus Himself interceded for His disciples and for all who would believe in Him (John 17). He also taught His followers to pray for their enemies (Matthew 5:44).

Contemplative Prayer: Contemplative prayer focuses on quieting the mind and entering into a deeper state of stillness and connection with the divine. It is a form of prayer that emphasizes listening, receiving insights, and experiencing a sense of unity with the divine. This prayer opens the hearts of the devotees and minds become calm like the surface water of an ocean without waves. Such types of prayer need regular practice and devotion.

Confession and Repentance: Everyone is prone to wrong actions and wrong attitudes toward others. When he realizes the wrongdoing, he takes the refuge of God for pardon. Confessional prayer involves acknowledging and seeking forgiveness for his mistakes, shortcomings, and transgressions. It is a form of prayer that promotes self-reflection, accountability, and the intention to make amends.

Benefits of Prayer:

Prayer offers various benefits on a personal and spiritual level:

- **Sense of Connection and Guidance**: Prayer provides a means to connect with the divine and seek guidance, comfort, and support in times of need. It can foster a sense of reassurance and hope. It provides you a sense of security that God is with you all the time and no injustice can happen to you in any circumstances.
- **Cultivation of Gratitude and Humility:** Prayer encourages the expression of gratitude and fosters a sense of humility, recognizing that there is a higher power beyond oneself. The entire creation is the product of the almighty. He is everything to his devotees. When the devotee realizes that his knowledge, power, and resources are limited without the blessings of the divine, he offers his deep devotion and gratitude to his divine god.
- **Spiritual Reflection and Growth:** Spiritual Reflection and Growth are very important aspects of life. Prayer facilitates self-reflection, introspection, and spiritual growth. It can deepen one's understanding of oneself, the divine, and the purpose of life.
- **Emotional and Mental Well-being:** Humans are emotional beings as they

understand their situation in society, acknowledge devotion, love, passion, hatred, and betrayal, etc. Engaging in prayer can promote emotional well-being by providing a space for expressing and processing emotions in a better way. It can also bring a sense of peace, calmness, and clarity to the mind.

- **Connection with a Community:** For those who engage in communal prayer, it fosters a sense of belonging and connection with others who share similar beliefs and values. Religious institutions like churches, mosques, temples, gurdwaras, etc. create space for the connection of masses with the divine god.

Personalized and Universal:

Prayer can be highly personalized, allowing individuals to express their unique beliefs, experiences, and needs. It can also be a universal practice that transcends specific religious or cultural boundaries, as it taps into the innate human longing for spiritual connection.

It's important to note that prayer is subjective and can take on different forms and meanings for different individuals. It is a deeply personal practice that can yield results. Without unwavering faith in the lotus feet of God, your prayer may not be accepted by Him. If your prayer is not heard your exercises become futile. However, don't lose your heart, continue your prayer, your mind, and heart will be united in due course of time and it will create unwavering faith in God. Never forget that God is your creator and knows everything about your needs, strengths, and weaknesses.

Contemplation

"The ultimate value of life depends upon awareness and the power of contemplation rather than upon mere survival." - Aristotle

Contemplation is a practice of deep reflection, introspection, and inner observation. It involves engaging the mind in focused and sustained attention to explore profound questions, spiritual or philosophical ideas, or the nature of reality. Contemplation is often associated with seeking wisdom, insight, and a deeper understanding of oneself and the world.

Some Key Points of Contemplation:

Intentional Reflection: Contemplation goes beyond ordinary thinking or casual reflection. It involves deliberately setting aside time and space for deep reflection and introspection. It is a purposeful practice of exploring and contemplating ideas, experiences, or concepts that hold significance to the individual.

Silence and Stillness: Contemplation can be reflected in a quiet and calm environment, without any distractions. The practice may involve sitting in solitude or engaging in activities that promote a state of inner stillness, peace, and silence. Creating a natural peaceful atmosphere helps to foster a deeper level of focus and concentration.

Inquiry and Exploration: Contemplation involves asking profound questions, exploring existential or spiritual themes, and contemplating the nature of reality, consciousness, or the self. It is a process of engaging the mind in deep inquiry and reflection, seeking insight, understanding, and a broader perspective. The body also plays a vital role in the contemplation of self, as it is the medium of realization of everything.

Non-Judgmental Observation: Contemplation requires an attitude of non-judgmental observation. Instead of seeking immediate answers or rushing to conclusions, contemplation involves observing thoughts, emotions, and experiences without attaching labels or judgments. It is about cultivating a sense of curiosity, openness, and acceptance. Contemplation needs time to shape the self-image for acceptance.

Contemplative Practices:

Contemplation can be practiced in various ways, depending on personal preferences and beliefs. Some common contemplative practices include:

- *Contemplative Reading*: Engaging in thoughtful reading of spiritual texts, philosophical writings, or poetry that provoke deep reflection and insight.
- *Reflective Writing:* Keeping a journal or engaging in reflective writing to explore thoughts, feelings, experiences, or philosophical ideas in a more structured and introspective manner.

- *Nature Contemplation*: Spending time in nature, observing and contemplating the beauty, patterns, and interconnectedness of the natural world. Never forget nature has every healing power for you.
- *Mindful Contemplation:* Combining elements of mindfulness and contemplation, where one focuses on the present moment and deeply reflects on a chosen theme or question.
- *Visual Contemplation*: Engaging in the observation and contemplation of art, symbols, or sacred imagery to evoke deep reflection and connection with deeper meanings.

Benefits of Contemplation:

Contemplation offers numerous benefits on a personal, intellectual, and spiritual level:

- *Enhanced Self-Awareness*: Contemplation facilitates self-reflection, introspection, and self-discovery. It can pave the way for one's understanding of personal values, beliefs, motivations, and patterns of behavior.
- *Inner Peace and Calm*: Engaging in contemplation can bring a sense of peace, tranquility, and inner calmness. It allows individuals to detach from external distractions and connect with their inner wisdom.
- *Expanded Perspective:* Contemplation encourages the exploration of different viewpoints, challenging assumptions, and expanding one's understanding of complex ideas or concepts.

- *Emotional Well-being:* Contemplation provides a space for exploring and processing emotions, fostering emotional resilience, and promoting a sense of acceptance and compassion toward oneself and others.
- *Spiritual Growth:* Contemplation is often associated with spiritual growth and the deepening of one's connection to the sacred or transcendent. It can lead to profound insights, a sense of awe, and a broader understanding of the nature of existence.

Contemplation is a personal and subjective practice. It allows individuals to engage in deep reflection and inquiry in a way that resonates with their unique beliefs, experiences, and aspirations. It can be an enriching inner powerhouse of the individual practitioner. Unless you engage in such spiritual actions you can't gain an actual idea about it. At times it is challenging but it can often also change your mental ecosystem and perception of the world around you.

Mindfulness

"Mindfulness is the awareness that arises from paying attention, on purpose, in the present moment, without judgment." - Jon Kabat-Zinn

Mindfulness plays a significant role in fostering a sense of God consciousness or spiritual awakening. It is a practice that involves paying attention to the present moment, with a non-judgmental and accepting attitude. By cultivating mindfulness, individuals can deepen their connection with the divine and enhance their awareness of the divine presence within and around them. While specific examples from epics and religious scriptures may vary depending on the tradition or belief system, the general principles of mindfulness can be found across various spiritual teachings.

Bhagavad Gita (Hinduism): In the Bhagavad Gita, Lord Krishna emphasizes the importance of mindfulness in the path of spirituality. He encourages Arjun, the warrior, to be fully present and focused in the present moment, detached from the outcomes of his actions. This state of mindfulness allows Arjun to connect with the divine and perform his duties without attachment. By being mindful, one can cultivate a deeper awareness of the divine presence and surrender to a higher power. Here is an example from Bhagavad Gita-

सुखदुःखे समे कृत्वा लाभालाभौ जयाजयौ।
ततो युद्धाय युज्यस्व नैवं पापमवाप्स्यसि॥ गीता ॥ 2.38 ॥

sukha-duḥkhe same kṛtvā lābhālābhau jayājayau
tato yuddhāya yujyasva naivaṁ pāpam avāpsyasi

In this verse, Lord Krishna advises Arjun to maintain equanimity in the face of pleasure and pain, success and failure, victory and defeat. Be present in the moment and forget about the past or future. *He encourages Arjun to fulfill his duties on the battlefield without being attached to the outcomes, as true fulfillment lies in performing one's responsibilities without any selfish desires or concerns.* Krishna assures Arjun that by adopting this attitude, *he will not accumulate negative karma or sin.*

Bible (Christianity): The Bible mentions several instances where mindfulness is portrayed as a means of drawing closer to God. For example, Psalm 46:10, says, ***"Be still, and know that I am God."*** This verse highlights the importance of stillness and inner calm as a way to connect with the divine presence. By practicing mindfulness and being present at the moment, individuals can experience a deeper sense of God's presence in their lives.

Sufi Poetry (Islam): Sufi poets often use **metaphors and imagery** to convey the essence of mindfulness and its connection to God-consciousness. The mystical poems of Rumi, for instance, emphasize the importance of awareness and presence. One of his famous verses states, ***"The quieter you become, the more you can hear."*** This verse illustrates how silence and stillness through mindfulness can open the doors of perception to connect with the divine.

Buddhism: Buddhism places great emphasis on mindfulness as a path to enlightenment. The practice of Zazen, or seated meditation, is central to Zen practice. By sitting in meditation and observing the breath and thoughts without judgment, practitioners cultivate mindfulness and develop a deep awareness of the present moment. This awareness can lead to a direct experience of the interconnectedness of all things, including a sense of transcendence or realization of the divine.

In summary, *mindfulness is a practice that can enhance one's sense of God consciousness by cultivating present-moment awareness, stillness, and acceptance.* In mindfulness practices, individuals can develop a deeper connection with the divine and experience the presence of God in their daily lives. The examples from various religious scriptures and traditions illustrate the significance of mindfulness in fostering a spiritual awakening and attaining a sense of God consciousness.

Chapter Five

The Role of Gratitude

Understanding the Power of Gratitude

"Gratitude turns what we have into enough, and more. It turns denial into acceptance, chaos into order, confusion into clarity... It makes sense of our past, brings peace for today, and creates a vision for tomorrow." - Melody Beattie

Understanding the power of gratitude is significant in everybody's life. It recognizes and acknowledges the significance of being grateful for the positive aspects of life, the kindness of others, and the blessings we receive. It is more than just saying **"thank you"** superficially. *In a true sense, it involves deep feeling and appreciation of the good things in our lives, both big and small.* Gratitude is a transformative product of a powerful mindset that can have profound effects on our well-being, relationships, and overall outlook on life including God consciousness.

The Gospel of Matthew in Holy Scripture says- ***"Whoever has gratitude will be given more, and he or she will have an abundance. Whoever does not have gratitude, even what he or she has will be taken from him or her."***

Further, the Bible Says- *"Enter his gates with thanksgiving and his courts with praise; give thanks to him and praise his name."* - Psalm 100:4.

 Lord Krishna in Gita says- *"He who is content with what he has, and rejoices in the Supreme Self, he is the greatest yogi."* - *Bhagavad Gita 6:18*

The above quote teaches us that gratitude is a key ingredient to spiritual fulfillment. When we are grateful for what we have, we are less likely to be attached to material possessions and more likely to focus on our inner journey. We are also more likely to experience joy and peace, even in the midst of difficult circumstances.

Growth Mindset:

Gratitude helps shift our focus from what we lack to what we have. Instead of dwelling on problems and shortcomings, we learn to see the positive aspects of our lives. This growth mindset can lead to increased happiness and contentment. It increases the inner peace of self rather than running after a mirage of uncertainty and ignorance. Accept the good things that you have, and thank them for the same rather than asking for more. *"Give thanks to the Lord in everything; for this is the will of God in Christ Jesus for you."* - *Thessalonians 5:18*

Emotional Well-being:

Expressing gratitude is linked to improved emotional well-being. It can reduce feelings of stress, anxiety, and depression. When you start practicing gratitude for everything like the beautiful sky, morning, cloud, nature, grass, a cup of tea, or a nice rose you will definitely feel relaxed. You will feel proud that nature has given you enough energy and freedom to enjoy. Enough resources to cherish, enough joy to be celebrated. Unless you admire and feel proud of the gift you have, you may not be able to get more as indicated earlier. When we count our blessings, we tend to experience more positive emotions and a greater sense of fulfillment. On the path to God consciousness, gratitude to Him is the fundamental chapter of the book of enlightenment.

Improved Relationship:

Grateful individuals are often more compassionate, empathetic, and understanding in their interactions with others. Expressing gratitude toward friends, family, and colleagues can strengthen relationships and foster a sense of connection. A good relationship means the creation of a good environment for success. A grateful man is often blessed by God and feels every heart is the temple of God. Everyone is a spirit or soul. Swami Vivekananda rightly says- ***"Worship of spirit by the spirit."***

Resilience:

Gratitude can enhance our ability to cope with challenges and setbacks. When we focus on what we are grateful for, we develop resilience and find the strength to overcome difficulties. It is the sincere gratitude of an individual that strengthens the inner being for more resilience in the social as well as spiritual arena.

Physical Health Benefits:

Studies have shown that practicing gratitude is associated with improved physical health. Grateful individuals may experience better sleep, lower blood pressure, and a stronger immune system. Grateful people are found less rigid less unhappy and more cheerful keeping their minds in happy mode. A happy mind means a happy and healthy physical body. An unhappy mind invites many diseases, causing the body to harbingers of viruses, bacteria, etc. A physically fit can search for ultimate knowledge like spiritual truth and search for the existence of God everywhere.

Reduced Materialism:

Gratitude helps counteract the consumerist mindset that often leads to chasing material possessions for happiness. Instead, it cultivates contentment with what we already have. For survival and to live long with love, affection, respect, and happiness we must have material assets. But all material aspects of life should not overshadow our spiritual awareness. Let your mind be satisfied with the existing material muse, and go in search of the ultimate truth the god consciousness.

Altruism and Generosity:

Gratitude is often linked to a desire to give back and help others. When we feel grateful for what we have, we are more likely to extend kindness and generosity to those in need. *"Being happy to help"* is a great quality in men that makes God happy. This is the reason, it is said **"service to mankind is service to god."** A grateful man is satisfied from within. A satisfied individual can be generous to everybody. He has the understanding that God is present everywhere as told by Krishna in Bhagavad Gita **"samo'haṁ sarvabhūteṣu"**

Mindfulness and Presence:

Gratitude encourages us to be present and mindful of the current moment. By being present in the moment, we can serve the nation better and get a better appreciation for ourselves increasing our self-esteem and confidence. When we do any work mindfully, we get better results. Such type of intense and mindful action is needed for God realization and understanding of His actions.

Spiritual Growth:

Gratitude is an essential aspect of many spiritual and religious traditions. It fosters a sense of humility, connection to a higher power, and appreciation for the mysteries of life. Gratitude connects everything in nature, you, me, all humans, the sun, moon, Planets, sky, earth, animals, and God. It removes the wall of ego, illusion and ignorance among us and leads to the path to God consciousness.

"In a state of God consciousness, there exists no division between the self and the divine. It is the recognition that we are all interlinked and integral components of a greater unity." - Eckhart Tolle

Practicing gratitude can take various forms, such as keeping a gratitude journal, expressing thanks to others, or simply taking a moment each day to reflect on the things we are grateful for. By incorporating gratitude into our lives, we can experience its transformative power, cultivate a more positive and fulfilling existence, and shape our objectives toward God realization.

How Gratitude Can Help Us Connect with God

Gratitude can play a significant role in connecting with God or a higher power for those who have a spiritual or religious belief system. Let us exploit together how gratitude can help us connect with God:

1. **Recognition of Blessings:** Expressing gratitude involves acknowledging and appreciating the blessings and gifts in our lives. By recognizing that these blessings come from a higher power or source, we develop a sense of humility and awe, deepening our connection with God. In the bible, it has been recognized in many ways. For example, Psalm 103:1-2*: "Bless*

the Lord, O my soul; and all that is within me, bless his holy name! Bless the Lord, O my soul, and forget not all his benefits."

In Hanuman Chalisa in Hindu Religious script, such blessings have been recognized with gratitude.   Hanuman is regarded as an incarnation of Lord Shiva and the best devotee of Lord Rama.

पावनतनया संकट हरन।

मंगला मूरति रूप।

राम लखन सीता सहित।

हृदय बसहु सुर भूप॥

Pāvanatanayā sankata harana।

Mangala Murati Roop।

Rāma Lakhana Sītā Sahita।

Hṛdaya Basahu Surabhūp॥

The above verse says "O Son of the Wind, the remover of distress, and jeopardy an embodiment of auspiciousness and divine form, you reside in the hearts of gods, With Lord Rama, Lakshmana, and Sita."

2. **Cultivating Humility:** Gratitude fosters humility by reminding us that we are not self-sufficient and that there are forces beyond our control that contribute to our well-being. This humility opens our hearts and minds to a higher power and enables us to surrender our egos in

the presence of the divine. Unless we understand our limitations, can't acknowledge the presence of a supreme being with us. It is the power of gratitude that refines us to that potential.

3. **Deepening Trust and Faith:** Gratitude nurtures trust and faith in God. When we express gratitude for the blessings we have received, it strengthens our belief that there is a benevolent force guiding and providing for us. This trust and faith deepen our connection with God as we surrender to His wisdom and divine plan. When we surrender, nothing leaves us to act, He is left in the driver's seat to run our lives' vehicles.

4. **Prayer and Gratitude:** Gratitude can be integrated into prayer as a way of expressing appreciation for the blessings and guidance received. It adds a dimension of thankfulness to our prayers and helps us connect with God on a deeper level, fostering a sense of intimacy and connection. In Deuteronomy 8:18 it is said: ***"But remember the Lord your God, for it is he who gives you the ability to produce wealth, and so confirms his covenant, the oath he swore to your ancestors, as it is today."*** Prayer is also one form of gratitude offered to God by the divine self.

5. **Presence and Mindfulness**: Gratitude encourages us to be present in the moment and mindful of the gifts and wonders of life. When we cultivate gratitude, we become more aware of

the divine presence in our everyday experiences, connecting with God in the beauty of nature, acts of kindness, or moments of grace. Mindfulness is the greatest treasure of a devotee to connect with God and to get his blessings. When it is partners with gratitude it makes wonders in the lives of the believers.

6. **Gratitude as a Spiritual Practice:** Making gratitude a regular spiritual practice deepens our connection with God. Setting aside time for gratitude meditation, reflection, or journaling allows us to focus our attention on the blessings and grace in our lives, creating a sacred space for communion with God. It is the gratitude that makes us closer to a spiritual connection with God. I can say with goodness, that an ungrateful individual can't get the path to God consciousness, because the ungrateful has no *bhakti* or devotion in his heart. Without devotion, one can't get the path to enlightenment.

7. **Surrender and Alignment:** Gratitude helps us align our hearts and minds with God's will. When we express gratitude for the blessings and challenges alike, we acknowledge that everything is part of a greater plan. This surrender and alignment with God's purpose strengthen our connection and deepen our trust in His guidance and bigger plan for us.

8. **Service and Generosity:** Gratitude often inspires acts of service and generosity toward

others. By extending kindness and sharing our blessings with those in need, we embody the spirit of gratitude and become conduits of God's love and compassion, strengthening our connection with Him. The Holy Scripture Bible has a lot to say about service to mankind in need. In fact, Jesus himself said that he came ***"not to be served but to serve"*** (Mark 10:45). And he taught his followers to do the same.

9. **Gratitude in Scripture and Religious Teachings**: Many religious texts and teachings emphasize the importance of gratitude in fostering a relationship with God. They highlight the transformative power of gratitude in deepening faith, promoting spiritual growth, and nurturing a connection with the divine. In Chapter 18, Verse 66 of the Bhagavad Gita Lord Krishna says;

सर्वधर्मान् परित्यज्य मामेकं शरणं व्रज।

अहं त्वां सर्वपापेभ्यो मोक्षयिष्यामि मा शुचः॥ गीता

"sarva-dharmān parityajya
    mām ekaṁ śaraṇaṁ vraja
ahaṁ tvāṁ sarva-pāpebhyo
    mokṣayiṣyāmi mā śucah"

In this verse, Krishna says ***"Whoever will surrender before me leaving all the egos and belief system at bay I will give him salvation. You may not have any second thoughts in your mind"***. The message of the verse is if you are obliged to your god, He is here to lift you and emancipate you from the shackles of all your sins and give you salvation.

The Bible, Ephesians 5:20: says ***"Giving thanks always and for everything to God the Father in the name of our Lord Jesus Christ."*** This verse tells us that we should give thanks to God for everything, always, and shall not forget it anyway.

Understanding the power of gratitude in the context of God consciousness is a profound concept that involves recognizing and acknowledging the significance of being grateful to the divine or a higher power. *The endpoint of gratitude to God is mental peace and happiness that makes wonder in the life of the devotee.* Overall, understanding the power of gratitude in God consciousness goes beyond a simple expression of thanks. It becomes a way of life, a transformative practice that elevates your consciousness, fosters inner peace, and aligns you with the higher purpose of existence. It is a powerful tool for personal growth, spiritual development, and living a fulfilling and meaningful life.

It's important to note that the experience of connecting with God through gratitude is deeply personal and can vary across individuals and belief systems. The key is to cultivate a sincere gratitude practice that resonates with your spiritual beliefs and allows you to cultivate a deeper connection with the divine.

Practical Tips for Cultivating Gratitude

Cultivating gratitude is a practice that can be integrated into our daily lives to enhance our overall well-being and foster a positive mindset. The practice can make anyone more relaxed, more acknowledged and more spiritual leading to clarity of God. You may likely follow some practical tips for cultivating gratitude:

Gratitude Journal: Keep a gratitude journal where you write down things you are grateful for each day. Take a few minutes in the morning or evening to reflect on the positive aspects of your life and jot them down. Be specific and focus on both big and small blessings. Never forget that every happening is the wish of God. He is the director and producer of Your Life drama. He is your entry point and end point and without His blessing, you are nowhere.

Morning Gratitude Practice: Start your day with a gratitude practice. Before getting out of bed, take a moment to mentally express gratitude for three things. It can be as simple as the gift of a new day, the warmth of your bed, or the love of your family. You may give thanks for more than three things like a beautiful morning, a wonderful sky, or frost on the grass. You may also offer gratitude to God for providing another beautiful day for action etc.

Expressing Gratitude to Others: Take some time to express your gratitude to people who have positively impacted your life. Write a thank-you note, send a heartfelt email, or express your appreciation in person. You may simply give thanks to your lovely mother, caring sister, or your darling father. If married never forget to thank your beloved wife. Let them know how their actions or presence has made a difference in your life.

Gratitude Walks: While you are enjoying a walk, intentionally focus on the things you are grateful for in your surroundings. Observe the beauty of nature, the sounds of birds chirping, or the warmth of the sun. Allow yourself to fully experience and appreciate the present moment. Give thanks to everything which have enriched your life small or big. Both have made you happy and strongly added value to your life. When offer your gratitude for everything you have and enjoy you feel very relaxed and obliged. An obliged heart is the temple of God you may not forget about it.

Meal Time Gratitude: Before starting your meals, pause for a moment to express gratitude for the food on your plate. Acknowledge the effort and resources that went into its production and express appreciation for the nourishment it provides. Make it your habit to suit your daily routine.

Gratitude Meditations: Incorporate gratitude into your meditation practice. During your meditation, intentionally bring to mind the things you are grateful for. Direct your attention to the sensations and emotions associated with gratitude. It can direct your mind toward the greatness of God. You can also use guided gratitude meditation apps or recordings for the purpose.

Gratitude Reminder: Set up reminders throughout your day to pause and reflect on something you are grateful for. It could be an alarm on your phone, a sticky note on your desk, or a visual cue like a gratitude stone or bracelet. Use these reminders to bring you back to the present moment and cultivate gratitude.

Shift Perspective in Challenges: Practice reframing challenges or difficult situations by finding the lessons or opportunities for growth within them. Look for silver linings or aspects you can be grateful for, even amidst adversity. This helps cultivate resilience and gratitude in the face of challenges.

Gratitude with Bedtime Reflection: Before going to sleep, reflect on three good things that happened during the day. Recall moments of joy, kindness, or progress. Allow yourself to relive those positive experiences and feel a sense of gratitude before drifting off to sleep.

Mindful Appreciation: Develop a habit of mindfully appreciating the present moment throughout your day. Pause and pay attention to the small joys and simple pleasures that often go unnoticed, such as the warmth of a cup of tea, a beautiful sunset, or a kind gesture from a stranger.

Remember that cultivating gratitude is an ongoing practice. It takes time and consistency to develop a gratitude mindset. By incorporating these practical tips into your daily life, you can gradually cultivate a greater sense of gratitude and experience the positive benefits it brings. Ultimately your soul will be pure and you will be inching toward the inner peace and the ultimate goal of God realization.

Chapter Six

The Power of Love

The Role of Love in Spiritual Growth

"Love is patient, love is kind. It does not envy, it does not boast, it is not proud. It does not dishonor others, it is not self-seeking, it is not easily angered, and it keeps no record of wrongs. Love does not delight in evil but rejoices with the truth. It always protects, always trusts, always hopes, and always perseveres."- Corinthians 13:4-7 in the New International Version (NIV) of the Bible.

This passage emphasizes the selfless and enduring nature of love. It describes love as being patient and kind, not seeking its interests or holding grudges. Love is not envious or proud, and it does not boast about itself. Instead, it honors others and is considerate of their feelings.

Love is also characterized by its ability to forgive and not be easily angered. It doesn't take pleasure in wrongdoing or deception but finds joy in the truth. Love is protective, trusting, hopeful, and persevering, even in the face of challenges and difficulties.

The role of love in spiritual growth is significant and multifaceted. Love can be seen as a transformative force that deepens our spiritual connection, expands our consciousness, and guides us toward self-realization. It plays a crucial role in various aspects of spiritual growth, including developing compassion, fostering unity, cultivating gratitude, and nurturing a connection with the divine. Let's explore these aspects in detail:

Developing Compassion:

Love is the foundation of compassion, which is an essential quality for spiritual growth. When we cultivate love, it opens our hearts to empathize with and understand the suffering of others. Through compassion, we learn to alleviate pain and contribute positively to the well-being of others. This process of caring for others helps us transcend our ego and expand our spiritual consciousness. When we truly love and care for someone, we naturally feel compassion toward them. For instance, a mother's love for her child enables her to empathize with the child's needs, feelings, and struggles. This love and compassion drive her to provide the necessary care and support. Such types of feelings with the intensity needed toward God. The love of Mother *Yosoda* toward Krishna, and the love of Hanuman toward Lord Ram are bright examples in this context.

Fostering Unity:

Love has the power to dissolve barriers and create a sense of unity and interconnectedness. It breaks down the illusion of separation and promotes a deep understanding that we are all interconnected beings. Love encourages us to recognize the divinity in others and treat everyone with respect and kindness. For example, when we approach others with love and see the divine essence within them, we build bridges of understanding and foster harmonious relationships. This unity-based love is not limited to personal connections but extends to embracing all living beings as part of the same interconnected web of life.

Cultivating Gratitude:

Love is intimately connected with gratitude. When we approach life with love, we develop an attitude of appreciation and gratitude for the blessings and experiences that come our way. Gratitude helps us stay present and mindful, recognizing the beauty and abundance in every moment. ***Divine love is unconditional and always available without any return.*** Gratitude is always associated with love and compassion and is inseparable.

Nurturing Connection with the Divine:

Love serves as a bridge between the individual and the divine. It enables us to establish a deep and intimate connection with a higher power or spiritual essence. When we approach spirituality with love, we experience a profound sense of unity, peace, and guidance from the divine. For example, ***through practices such as prayer, meditation, or devotional rituals, individuals often express their love for the divine.*** These acts of devotion foster a deeper relationship with the divine and facilitate spiritual growth. When someone has the essential knowledge of God's presence everywhere, he will automatically love everything.

Transformation and Healing:

Love has the power to transform and heal. It can dissolve barriers, resentments, and conflicts, fostering forgiveness, reconciliation, and inner healing. *When individuals open their hearts to love, they create space for personal growth, emotional healing, and spiritual transformation.* He becomes the limitless lover of every creation of the universe.

Unconditional Acceptance:

Love encompasses unconditional acceptance and non-judgment. It allows individuals to accept themselves and others as they are, embracing both strengths and weaknesses. Through love's acceptance, individuals can experience a profound sense of belonging and worthiness, contributing to their spiritual growth. An example from the Bhagavad Gita, which highlights the above concept of unconditional acceptance.

समः शत्रौ च मित्रे च तथा मानापमानयोः।
शीतोष्णसुखदुःखेषु समः सङ्गविवर्जितः॥ Gita.12.18 ॥

Samaha śatrau cha mitre cha tathā mānāpamānayoḥ
Śītoṣṇa-sukha-duḥkheṣu samaha saṅgavivarjitaḥ.

In the above verse, Lord Krishna describes the qualities of a devotee who has reached the highest state of equanimity and detachment. Such a person remains unaffected by the dualities of life, whether it's pleasure or pain, honor or dishonor, hot or cold. They treat friends and enemies at par, maintaining a balanced and serene mind. This state of inner balance and detachment is considered to be a sign of advanced spiritual maturity and devotion.

Transcending Dualities:

Love helps individuals transcend dualities and embrace unity consciousness. It goes beyond divisions such as good and bad, self and other, and fosters a sense of unity and harmony. Through love, individuals can recognize the divine in all beings, cultivating a broader perspective and spiritual growth. **A verse from the Bhagavad Gita justifies it.**

"समोऽहं सर्वभूतेषु न मे द्वेष्योऽस्ति न प्रियः।
ये भजन्ति तु मां भक्त्या मयि ते तेषु चाप्यहम्॥" Gita ||9.29||

samo'ham sarvabhūteṣu na me dveṣyo'sti na priyaḥ
ye bhajanti tu māṁ bhaktyā mayi te teṣu cāpy aham

In the Bible, such a concept has been mentioned in many places. Let us refer to one example; Jeremiah 23:23-24: *"Am I only a God close at hand," declares the Lord, "and not a God far away? 'Can anyone hide in secret places so I cannot see them?' declares the Lord. 'Do not I fill heaven and earth?"* (This verse emphasizes that

God's presence fills all of creation, leaving no place beyond his reach.)

Inner Transformation:

Love is a catalyst for inner transformation. When individuals cultivate love within themselves, it can dissolve negative patterns, heal emotional wounds, and lead to personal growth. Love helps individuals awaken to their true nature and align with their highest potential, contributing to their spiritual development. Inner transformation opens the door for God realization. A transformed heart is the dwelling place of love, compassion, tolerance, patience, and gratitude, which are loving terms of God.

Integration of Wisdom:

Love integrates wisdom and knowledge into action. It allows individuals to embody and live their spiritual principles, translating spiritual insights into compassionate action. Love ensures that spiritual growth is not merely intellectual or theoretical but manifests in practical ways in one's relationships, interactions, and contributions to the world.

Fulfillment and Joy:

Love brings a sense of fulfillment and joy. When individuals live in alignment with love, they experience a deep sense of purpose, contentment, and joy. Love becomes a guiding force that infuses life with meaning and enriches the spiritual journey.

In summary, love plays a vital role in spiritual growth by developing compassion, fostering unity, cultivating gratitude, and nurturing a connection with the divine. Through love, we expand our consciousness, transcend our ego, and align ourselves with the deeper truths of existence. By embracing love in our spiritual journey, we can experience profound transformation and contribute to the well-being of ourselves and others.

Loving Oneself

The role of loving oneself in God consciousness is an important aspect of spiritual growth and self-realization. When we talk about loving oneself in this context, it goes beyond mere self-esteem or self-indulgence. It involves recognizing and honoring the divine essence within ourselves and cultivating a deep sense of self-acceptance, compassion, and reverence. Let us explore the role of loving oneself in God consciousness together:

Recognizing the Divine Within:

Loving oneself in God consciousness begins with acknowledging the presence of the divine within us. We are spiritual beings having a human experience, and our true nature is rooted in the divine essence. By loving ourselves, we are essentially honoring the divine spark that resides within us.

For Example: Imagine looking at yourself in the mirror and seeing beyond your physical appearance. Remember the physical body is the temple, where the divine soul resides. You recognize the divine presence that dwells within your being—the eternal and unchanging essence that is connected to the source of all creation. Without divine presence, we are no longer alive.

The Bible (Ecclesiastes 12:7:) says; ***"Then the dust will return to the earth as it was, and the spirit will return to God who gave it."***

This verse explains that a human being is composed of both the physical body (dust) and a spiritual essence (spirit) that originates from and ultimately returns to God.

One verse from the Bhagavad Gita justifies the above truth of the divine presence within us.

द्विविमौ पुरुषौ लोके क्षरश्चाक्षर एव च।

क्षरः सर्वाणि भूतानि कूटस्थोऽक्षर उच्यते॥ Gita.15.16 ॥

dvavimau puruṣau loke kṣaraścākṣara eva ca
kṣaraḥ sarvāṇi bhūtāni kūṭastho'kṣara ucyate

There are two types of beings in this world - perishable (*kṣara*) and imperishable (*akṣara*). The perishable represents the physical body of all living beings, while the imperishable is the unchanging eternal self, or soul unaffected by the cycle of birth and death.

Self-Acceptance and Compassion:

Loving one in God consciousness involves embracing all aspects of ourselves, including our strengths, weaknesses, and imperfections. It means accepting ourselves unconditionally and showing compassion toward our struggles and shortcomings. Through self-acceptance and compassion, we can heal and transform those parts of ourselves that may need nurturing and growth. Instead of being overly critical of our mistakes or shortcomings, we offer ourselves compassion and understanding. We recognize that we are on a journey of learning and growth. It is nothing to blame or worry about. There is a scope for us to treat ourselves with the same kindness and forgiveness that we would extend to others near and dear. *Accepting self means accepting the divine within us with respect and joy.*

Cultivating Inner Harmony:

Loving oneself in God consciousness means creating a state of inner harmony and peace. By nurturing self-love, we align our thoughts, actions, and intentions with the divine qualities of love, joy, and serenity. We prioritize self-care and engage in practices that nourish our mind, body, and soul.

Many activities such as meditation, spending time in nature, or engaging in creative pursuits can help us cultivate inner harmony and strengthen our connection with the divine. These practices allow us to listen to our inner voice, align with our true purpose, and live by our highest potential. Inner harmony can heal inner deficiencies, illness, and distracted mindset.

Expressing Divine Love:

When we love ourselves in God consciousness, we become channels for divine love to flow through us. *As we develop a deep sense of self-love, we naturally radiate love, kindness, and compassion toward others.*

Parker Palmer rightly says-***"Self-care is never a selfish act-it is simply good stewardship of the only gift I have, the gift I was put on earth to offer to others."*** Our actions and interactions are infused with divine qualities, and we become instruments of love in the world. *Divine love not only nurtures self but also enriches the lives of millions.*

Through acts of kindness, compassion, and service to others, we express the divine love that emanates from within us. We treat others with respect, empathy, and understanding, recognizing their inherent divinity, just as we recognize it within ourselves.

In summary, loving one in God consciousness involves recognizing the divine within, practicing self-acceptance and compassion, cultivating inner harmony, and expressing divine love in our interactions with others. As we embrace self-love in this profound way, we deepen our spiritual connection, align with our true nature, and contribute to the manifestation of love and unity in the world.

Loving Others

Loving others and God-consciousness are interconnected concepts that often go hand in hand, especially in the context of spiritual and religious beliefs. We can understand the relationship in the following paragraphs.

Loving Others:

Loving others refers to the act of extending care, compassion, and goodwill toward fellow human beings including the animals. It involves recognizing the inherent worth and value of every individual and treating them with kindness, respect, and empathy. This type of love is not limited to family or friends but extends to all people, including strangers, neighbors, and even those with whom we may disagree. Our nonviolent approach toward the animals also comes under such compassion. The bigger goodwill message of Vedic prayer is the brightest example of loving others.

सर्वे भवन्तु सुखिनः, सर्वे सन्तु निरामयाः।
सर्वे भद्राणि पश्यन्तु, मा कश्चित् दुःखभाग्भवेत्॥

Sarve bhavantu sukhinaḥ,
     sarve santu nirāmayāḥ.
Sarve bhadrāṇi paśyantu,
     mā kashchit duḥkhabhāgbhavet.

May all be happy, and may all be free from illness.
May all see auspiciousness, and may none suffer.

This verse is a well-known Vedic prayer for the well-being and happiness of all living beings. It expresses a heartfelt wish for the welfare of everyone, spreading love, and compassion. This prayer beautifully captures the essence of universal love, care, and compassion. It reflects the Indian tradition's emphasis on the welfare of all living beings and serves as a reminder of our interconnectedness and shared humanity and God consciousness. Buddhist spiritual scripture echoes the concept in the Vedic line. *"May all beings be happy and safe. May all beings be free from suffering. May all beings live in peace."*- Pali Canon: Metta Sutta (The Buddha's Discourse on Loving-Kindness):

God-consciousness:

God-consciousness, also known as spiritual awareness or mindfulness of the divine, refers to the state of being aware of and connected to a higher power or a transcendent reality. It involves recognizing the presence of a divine presence or energy in our lives and seeking to align our thoughts, actions, and intentions with spiritual principles or teachings.

The relationship between loving others and God-consciousness can be understood in the following ways:

a) Spiritual teachings: Many religious and spiritual traditions emphasize the importance of loving others as an integral part of one's spiritual journey. They often view love as a central virtue that reflects the divine nature and fosters spiritual growth and enlightenment. In the bible, it has been highlighted such as; *"Dear friends, let us love one another, for love comes from God. Everyone who loves has been born of God and knows God. Whoever does not love does not know God, for God is love. This is how God's love was revealed among us: God sent his one and only Son into the world so that we might live through him. In this is love, not that we loved God but that he loved us and sent his Son as an atoning sacrifice for our sins.*

Dear friends, since God so loved us, we also ought to love one another."- 1 John 4:7-11:

b) Connection to the divine: When we engage in acts of love and compassion toward others, we align ourselves with the principles and values that are often associated with a higher power or divine source. Loving others can be seen as an expression of our connection to that divine presence, reflecting the love and kindness we believe to be inherent in that higher power. The Bible says Jesus replied: ***"Love the Lord your God with all your heart and with all your soul and with all your mind.' This is the first and greatest commandment. And the second is like it: 'Love your neighbor as yourself."-*** Matthew 22:37-39:

c) Service and selflessness: Loving others involves selflessness and a willingness to put the needs and well-being of others before our own. This act of service and selflessness is often seen as a way to transcend the ego and cultivate a deeper connection with the divine. By loving others, we participate in the divine work of caring for creation and embodying the qualities that are considered godly or spiritual. The Hindu scriptures highlight selfless services as the foundation for spiritual growth and the realization of ultimate truth (*Brahman*).

d) Unity and interconnectedness: Many spiritual traditions teach that all beings are interconnected and part of a greater whole. When we love others, we acknowledge and honor this interconnectedness. This recognition of our shared humanity and the divine spark within each person helps cultivate a sense of unity and oneness, aligning us with the broader spiritual principles of love, compassion, and harmony. In the Upanishad, Chandogya Upanishad 6.10-11, we find the famous teaching of **"Tat Tvam Asi"** or "You are That." This teaching emphasizes the unity of all beings and the interconnectedness of all things. In the Bhagavad Gita, Chapter 6, Verse 30, Krishna says:

"यो मां पश्यति सर्वत्र सर्वं च मयि पश्यति

तस्याहं न प्रणश्यामि स च मे न प्रणश्यति"

"yo māṁ paśyati sarvatra sarvaṁ ca mayi paśyati
tasyāhaṁ na praṇaśyāmi sa ca me na praṇaśyati"

"Whoever sees Me in all beings and all beings in Me—he never becomes detached from Me, nor do I become detached from him."

The Quran also says the importance of unity and interconnectedness among humanity. ***"O mankind, indeed We created you from one male and one female and made you into nations and tribes that you may know one another. Indeed, the most noble of you in the sight of Allah is the most righteous of you. Indeed, Allah is Knowing and Acquainted."*** (Quran 49:13)

In summary, loving others and God-consciousness are intertwined concepts that reinforce each other. By practicing love and compassion toward others, we can deepen our spiritual awareness and connection to a higher power or spiritual reality. Likewise, cultivating God-consciousness can inspire and guide our acts of love and service toward others, fostering a more compassionate and meaningful existence.

Compassion and Empathy

"Empathy is the bridge that connects you to others. Compassion is the bridge that connects you to God." - Karen Kaigler-Walker

Compassion and empathy play vital roles in our spiritual journey. They are not only words but have the enormous power within to influence and do magic in others' lives. They connect with hearts, understand human emotions, and love themselves and others. Working with compassion and empathy contributes to spiritual growth:

Cultivating Oneness: Compassion and empathy help individuals recognize the inherent interconnectedness of all beings. *They dissolve the illusion of separation and foster a sense of unity and oneness with others, the natural world, and the divine.* This realization supports spiritual growth by nurturing a broader perspective and deepening one's connection to the larger web of existence. One Gospel of Luke from the Bible-**"Do to others whatever you would have them do to you."** (Luke 6:31) provides a clear picture of it. This passage, known as the Golden Rule, teaches us to treat others with the same compassion and empathy that we would want to be treated with. It is a reminder that we are all interconnected and that we should value others as much as we value ourselves.

When such feelings pour into our hearts, there will be no separate ego to attend.

#Deepening Self-Reflection: Compassion and empathy facilitate self-reflection by encouraging individuals to look within and understand their own emotions, motivations, and experiences. They create a space for introspection and self-inquiry, allowing individuals to gain insights into their suffering, struggles, and patterns of behavior. This self-awareness is a crucial component of spiritual growth. Unless you are aware of your self-worthiness, self-deficiencies, and self-acceptance you may not prepare yourself to proceed toward the spiritual arena.

Healing and Forgiveness: Let us see one of the most famous passages from the Gospel of Matthew: ***"Have compassion on one another; be kind to each other, forgiving each other, just as in Christ God forgave you."*** (Matthew 6:14) that highlights the message of forgiveness. Compassion and empathy are transformative forces that facilitate healing and forgiveness. They allow individuals to acknowledge and empathize with their pain and the pain of others. Through compassion, individuals can heal emotional wounds, release resentment, and cultivate forgiveness, leading to personal growth and liberation from emotional burdens. Forgiveness is the heavenly message everybody needs to exercise on the path to God consciousness.

Service and Altruism: Compassion and empathy inspire us to acts of service and altruism. They motivate individuals to extend care and support to others without expecting anything in return. In the Bhagavad Gita, it is stated that;

तस्मादसक्तः सततं कार्यं कर्म समाचर।
असक्तो ह्याचरन्कर्म परमाप्नोति पूरुषः।।3.19।।

One who performs his duties without attachment to the fruits of those actions is more likely to get spiritual growth through selfless service. He is more likely to get the blessings of God consciousness.

Examples of such types of selfless services are found in the Bible-
"Do nothing out of selfish ambition or vain conceit. Rather, in humility value others above yourselves, not looking to your own interests but each of you to the interests of the others." (Philippians 2:3-4, New International Version): This Bible verse from the book of Philippians emphasizes the idea of selflessness and placing the interests of others above one's own, highlighting the importance of serving others with humility and without selfish motives. Engaging in acts of service contributes to spiritual growth by fostering a sense of interconnectedness, cultivating humility, and expanding one's capacity to love and serve.

Transcending Judgment: Compassion and empathy involve suspending judgment and embracing a non-judgmental attitude toward oneself and others. They enable individuals to see beyond external appearances and labels, recognizing the common humanity and inherent worth in all beings. This non-judgmental stance fosters openness, acceptance, and deeper understanding, facilitating spiritual growth. Non-judgmental action opens one's heart to universal brotherhood and acceptance, which are great ways to happiness. Where is happiness, God is there because God likes happiness.

Heart-Opening and Love: Compassion and empathy open the heart, allowing individuals to experience and express love toward themselves and others. Love is considered a central force in spiritual growth, and compassion and empathy serve as pathways to accessing and embodying this love. Love brings joy, fulfillment, and a deeper connection with the divine, facilitating spiritual transformation.

Expansion of Consciousness: Compassion and empathy expand consciousness by broadening one's awareness beyond personal concerns and embracing the experiences and suffering of others. They cultivate a sense of universal compassion, inviting individuals to engage in the collective healing and transformation of humanity. This expanded consciousness is an integral aspect of spiritual growth.

Integration of Spiritual Teachings: Compassion and empathy allow individuals to integrate spiritual teachings into their daily lives. They provide a practical application of spiritual principles, translating them into compassionate actions and relationships. By embodying these qualities, individuals align their actions with their spiritual beliefs, fostering growth and transformation.

Connection with the Divine: On the path to connecting with the divine or higher energy, compassion and empathy play a very positive role. By embodying these qualities, individuals align themselves with the loving and compassionate nature of the divine. This alignment strengthens the spiritual bond and facilitates spiritual growth by opening the channels for divine guidance, grace, and transformative experiences.

Cultivating compassion and empathy is a lifelong journey that requires practice, self-reflection, and conscious effort. Through their cultivation, individuals can experience profound spiritual growth, deepening their connection with themselves, others, and the divine.

Chapter Seven

Overcoming Obstacles to God Consciousness

Common Obstacles to Spiritual Growth

On the path of spiritual growth, individuals may encounter various obstacles that can hinder their progress and understanding. Let us encounter together some common obstacles to spiritual growth that are observed in the lives of the people seeking God consciousness.

Ego Identification:

In the context of spirituality and philosophy, the term *"ego" refers to the sense of a separate and individual self. It often leads to a sense of self-importance, attachment, and identification with worldly desires and possessions.* Further, the ego is a sense of self that separates an individual from God and others. It is often characterized by pride and arrogance. The ego can be a powerful force in our lives, but it can also lead to suffering and disconnection. The ego is a veil that separates an individual from God. The human without ego and egoism are really blessed children of God. The concept of ego is addressed in various spiritual texts, including the Bhagavad Gita, an ancient Hindu scripture, the Bible, Buddhism, etc.

The Gita provides insights into understanding the nature of the ego and its implications for spiritual growth. It describes how individuals often become attached to their roles, possessions, and relationships, and develop a strong sense of *"I" and "mine."* This attachment leads to desires, expectations, and a sense of entitlement. Gita explains that the ego gives rise to the illusion of control. People with a strong sense of ego believe they are the sole doers of their actions and have complete control over the outcomes. However, the Gita teaches that the true nature of reality is much more complex, and various factors and forces are behind the scenes.

The Gita emphasizes the need to transcend the ego to realize our true spiritual nature as **we are born divine**. We are trapped by the nature of material desires. The Gita encourages selflessness, detachment, and the cultivation of a sense of surrender to a higher power or divine will. By letting go of the ego's desires and attachments, one can experience a deeper connection with the divine and attain spiritual liberation. In the context of the Bhagavad Gita, "ego" can be understood as a sense of self-identity or individuality that can often lead to attachment, desires, and delusion. It is referred to as *"ahamkara"* in Sanskrit, which translates to *"ego"* in English. Ego is also manifested in the form of pride and arrogance on the part of an individual.

Here is an example of a verse from the Bhagavad Gita that mentions the concept of ego:

यदा ते मोहकलिलं बुद्धिर्व्यतितरिष्यति।
तदा गन्तासि निर्वेदं श्रोतव्यस्य श्रुतस्य च॥ Gita ॥2.52॥

Yadā te moha-kalilaṁ buddhir vyatitarishyati,
Tadā gantāsi nirvedaṁ shrutavyasya shrutasya cha.

In this verse, Lord Krishna advises Arjun that when one's intellect transcends the delusion caused by the ego, one will become dispassionate and indifferent to the external influences of the world. This detachment allows a person to accept higher truths and gain spiritual insight beyond the materialistic desires influenced by the ego.

The Gita extols the virtues of humility and selflessness as antidotes to the ego. It encourages individuals to perform their duties without seeking personal gains or recognition. Instead, focus on serving others and working for the welfare of all. This shift in perspective helps diminish the ego's dominance and promotes a more harmonious and compassionate approach to life.

You can also find many references about the ego in the Bible. In the Gospel of Matthew, Jesus says: ***"Whoever wants to be my disciple must deny themselves and take up their cross and follow me."*** (Matthew 16:24). Further, the Bible strongly condemns pride and arrogance, often associated with an inflated ego. The following verses illustrate the same:

- Proverbs 16:18: ***"Pride goes before destruction, a haughty spirit before a fall."***

- James 4:6: ***"But he gives us even more grace; that is why it says, "God opposes the proud but gives grace to the humble."***

If you need God you have to let your ego at bay. Ego and God can't co-exist with you all together.

In Buddhism, the concept of the ego holds a central role in understanding the nature of suffering and the path to liberation. Within Buddhist philosophy, the ego is often referred to as the **"self"** or **"self-identity."** It is perceived as a profound illusion that serves as the root cause of attachment, craving, and ignorance. Rather than being a fixed and unchanging entity, the ego is viewed as a complex amalgamation of constantly shifting mental and physical components.

This illusory identification with the self gives rise to suffering and a pervasive sense of discontentment. However, ***Buddhism places great emphasis on the impermanence of all phenomena, including the ego.*** It is seen as a transient and ever-evolving construct, arising and dissolving in response to a multitude of causes and conditions.

In fact, in Buddhism, the ego is recognized as a **fleeting mirage, a mirage** having no permanent position. It only leads to suffering, but understanding its ephemeral nature is a vital step toward spiritual realization and liberation in Buddhism.

One significant obstacle is *the identification with the ego, the sense of a separate and individual self.* The ego tends to create a false sense of identity, attachment to material possessions, and a focus on personal desires and achievements. Overcoming this obstacle involves recognizing the transient nature of the ego and *cultivating a deeper understanding of the true self beyond the ego.*

Attachment and Desire:

Buddha says- ***"Attachment leads to suffering."*** He was the appropriate authority to justify his saying. Because he was a prince and left all pleasure, comfort, desires, and attachment to material pleasure in search of true knowledge and enlightenment. Attachment and excessive desire for material possessions, relationships, or specific outcomes can hinder spiritual growth. Attachment creates dependency on unreal possessions and prevents individuals from experiencing true freedom and inner peace. Overcoming this obstacle involves cultivating detachment, and recognizing the impermanence of external conditions. In practice, a penniless sanyasi or a saint enjoys happiness and enjoys sound sleep whereas a millionaire can have that due to the apprehension of theft of their wealth and the desire to get more possessions. The only desire left for him is to get spiritual insight, work for the entire humanity, and get salvation.

Lack of Self-Awareness:

A lack of self-awareness (who are you) can impede spiritual growth. It can prevent individuals from recognizing their patterns, conditioning, and limitations. Self-awareness is crucial for introspection, identifying areas for growth, and understanding the deeper aspects of oneself. In a spiritual journey, a **sadguru** or spiritual guide can guide you in achieving awareness. Other ways such as cultivating mindfulness, self-reflection, and a willingness to explore one's inner landscape can help overcome a lack of self-awareness.

Distractions and Busyness:

The modern world is filled with distractions and busyness that can divert individuals' attention from their spiritual journey. Constant engagement with technology, work-related responsibilities, and societal pressures can leave little time for introspection and inner growth. It is important to overcome this obstacle by creating space for solitude, silence, and mindful practices that allow you to reconnect with your inner self. Remember that "Where there's a will, there's a way." You have to find time for yourself only for spiritual growth and alignment with the divine.

Negative Conditioning and Beliefs:

Negative conditioning, societal beliefs, and limiting self-beliefs can hinder spiritual growth. These negative patterns of thinking and behavior can create barriers and restrict individuals from exploring new possibilities and expanding their consciousness. There are ways to transform limiting beliefs, into unlimited opportunities, develop unwavering faith in the divine entity, and embrace new perspectives. There is a scope for improvement in your life every minute and embrace a growth mindset of spiritual awakening. Your life is yours live in it with happiness for spiritual and personal growth. Never mind the criticism and unkind words of others about you, because you can't control what others say but align yourself as per your program.

Lack of Discipline and Consistency:

Inconsistent spiritual practices and a lack of discipline can impede progress on the spiritual path. Be regular and committed to cultivating spiritual qualities, and experiencing inner transformation. Consistent spiritual practices, setting intentions, and prioritizing time for growth and self-reflection are the ways to overcome the above drawbacks.

Judgment and Comparison:

Judgment of oneself and others, as well as constant comparison, can hinder spiritual growth. *Judgment and comparison reinforce the illusion of separation, create a sense of superiority or inferiority complexity, and generate disharmony within oneself and with others.* Cultivating compassion, empathy, non-judgment, and embracing the growth mindset can overcome such types of obstacles on the path to spiritual growth.

Lack of Guidance and Support:

The absence of spiritual guidance or a supportive community can be an obstacle to spiritual growth. If you are serious about having a spiritual self and God consciousness you have to enjoy the company of

Sadguru, spiritual mentors, or teachers. Lord Srikrishna during His valuable advice to Arjun says;

"Tad viddhi praṇipātena paripraśnena sevayā
Upadekṣyanti te jñānaṁ jñāninas tattva-darśinaḥ"
Gita || 4.34 ||

Learn that knowledge and wisdom from the wise self-realised seers or gurus through humble submission, inquiry, and relentless service.

It is a fact that the experienced and enlightened can provide guidance, and inspiration, which can greatly enhance your spiritual journey. Reading sacred texts, and attending spiritual lectures, and discourses can enhance your mental image of spiritual thoughts, perceptions, and acceptance.

It's important to note that these obstacles are not fixed barriers but rather opportunities for growth and learning. Overcoming these obstacles requires self-awareness, inner work for peace, and a commitment to the spiritual path. With perseverance and dedication, individuals can navigate these obstacles and continue to progress on their journey of spiritual growth.

Strategies for Overcoming Obstacles

Obstacles in our lives are temporary in nature. Understanding the nature of obstacles is the first step toward eradication. In the previous subheading, we encountered the nature of obstacles with the trailer of solutions. Here we shall discuss more in overcoming obstacles to God consciousness. We all are aware of the fact that life is not a bed of roses always but has some thorns in it and we have to proceed carefully. If infected by sharp thorns never blame God rather praise and offer gratitude for His mercy of being affected less. Opportunities and obstacles are part of life's journey and patience and faith in God is a pathfinder. The following strategies can help you to overcome obstacles and deepen your connection with God.

Self-Reflection and Awareness:

Cultivate self-awareness by regularly reflecting on your thoughts, emotions, and behaviors. The thinking process is the product of the mind, which is very unstable. When the mind is diverted from the specific ideas and emotions of the divine, you have to draw it to the specific point of attention repeatedly. In the Bhagavad Gita when Arjun asks lord Krishna, how to control the fickle mind, Krishna says; अभ्यासेन तु कौन्तेय वैराग्येण च गृह्यते। Gita ||6.35|| Through constant practice and detachment, from the material world, one can get control over an unstable mind. Identify the specific obstacles or patterns that hinder your progress toward God consciousness. This self-reflection helps you gain clarity on the areas that require attention and transformation.

Mindfulness and Presence:

Practice mindfulness to bring awareness to the present moment. Be present in the moment of divine service like worship of God, reading religious texts, chanting the guru mantra or any bija mantra, cleaning the sacred space, or participating in any religious gathering. ***In mindfulness practice, it is important to be an attentive listener of your own chanting, reading, etc.*** By being fully present, you can observe your thoughts, emotions, and reactions will gradually stabilize on the lotus feet of your God. This allows you to recognize and release the obstacles as they arise, fostering a deeper connection with God.

Surrender and Letting Go:

In God consciousness, completely surrender your ego, knowledge, social status, power, etc. before God. Behave as an innocent child not aware of the world around you, very happy as you were before your mother during childhood. Because God is everything to a devotee, mother, father, friend, philosopher, and many more. Remember God knows everything, about you, your past, present, and future and you can't hide anything from Him. Complete surrender is the only way to get his divine mercy and blessings. Prepare yourself to become open before him. He is very kind and forgives everybody irrespective of the character of the surrendered. Release all the attachments, expectations, and control over the material world onto Him. When you are free of unnecessary attachment you will get space for divine guidance and intervention. Trust in the higher plan and surrender to the flow of life.

Prayer and Meditation:

Engage in regular prayer and meditation practices to quiet the monkey mind. Avoid multitasking, give the mind some rest, and be happy. Open your heart, and deepen your connection with the divine. Prayer has enormous power and allows you to communicate with God, express your intentions, and seek guidance. In every faith, you can often find the space for prayer and meditation. Meditation helps cultivate inner peace, stillness, clarity, and receptivity to the divine presence.

Study and Contemplation:

Engage in the study of spiritual texts, teachings, and wisdom traditions that resonate with you. If not understood seek the guidance of your guru or spiritual guide. Reflect on the deeper meanings and contemplate their relevance in your life. This intellectual and contemplative exploration can provide insights, inspiration, and guidance on your path to God consciousness.

Seek Guidance and Support:

Seek guidance from spiritual mentors, teachers, or a supportive community. They can offer wisdom, support, and a sense of belonging. Surround yourself with like-minded individuals who share similar spiritual aspirations and can provide encouragement and inspiration. It is wise to take refuge in the lotus feet of the self-realized Sadguru, who can provide all necessary guidance to the path of God realization without any hesitation and asking for any return.

Cultivate Virtuous Qualities:

Focus on cultivating virtuous qualities such as compassion, kindness, selfless service, honesty, forgiveness, and gratitude. These qualities often help purify the mind and heart of the individual. Engage in acts of service and selflessness. By helping others and contributing to the well-being of others, you cultivate a sense of interconnectedness and deepen your connection with God. Serving others with love and compassion allows you to transcend self-centeredness and expand your capacity for divine consciousness. The phrase *"Service to mankind is service to God"* is a popular saying that emphasizes the importance of selfless service and helping others as a way to serve a higher purpose or the divine. In various religious and spiritual traditions, there is a strong emphasis on compassion, charity, and altruism as a means to connect with the divine and serve the greater good. The idea is that by serving and helping others, we are expressing our love and devotion to a higher power or God residing within them. This concept is present in different forms in various religious scriptures and teachings. For example, in Hinduism, there is the belief in **"Seva"** (selfless service) as a way to express devotion to God and attain spiritual growth. In Christianity, the Bible mentions in Matthew 25:40, ***"Truly I tell you, whatever you did for one of the least of these brothers and sisters of mine, you did for me."***
Virtuous qualities like selfless services create a conducive environment for God consciousness to flourish. Include them in your daily routine of interactions and relationships.

Cultivate Gratitude:

Practice gratitude by regularly expressing appreciation for the blessings in your life. Cultivating gratitude shifts your focus from scarcity to abundance, hate to love, enmity to friendship, opening your heart to the divine presence. Recognize and acknowledge the divine grace and blessings that surround you. Cultivating gratitude in God consciousness means being thankful and appreciative of the blessings and gifts received from the divine in our lives. One example of practicing gratitude in God consciousness is:

Imagine a person who faces a challenging situation in life, such as a serious illness or a difficult financial crisis. Instead of feeling overwhelmed by the situation, this person chooses to focus on the positive aspects of life and maintains faith in God's plan. He expresses his gratitude as follows-

"Dear God, (name of your personal God) I am going through a tough time, but I am grateful for the strength and resilience you have given me to face these challenges. I thank you for the love and support of my family and friends who stand by my side during this difficult journey. I am thankful for the lessons I am learning through this experience, which are helping me grow as a person. I trust in your divine wisdom and know that you have a purpose for everything that happens in my life. Thank you for guiding me and showering me with your blessings."

In this example, the person acknowledges the difficulties he is facing but chooses to focus on the positive aspects of his life, expressing gratitude for the support he has and trusting in the greater plan set forth by God. This practice of gratitude in God consciousness can bring comfort, peace, and a sense of connection to the divine, even during challenging times.

Patience and Persistence:

God tests your patience. You can find many stories of devotees in sacred texts, who have undergone many challenges but got divine blessings. Be resilient to the divine journey. Spiritual growth is a lifelong journey, and progress may not always be linear. Trust in the process, be patient with yourself, have faith in divine planning, and persist in your spiritual practices even during challenging times.

Remember that everyone's journey is unique, and it's important to find the strategies that resonate with you. Be patient in your approach and make you a true **Bhakta**/ diehard devotee. Embrace your obstacles as opportunities for growth and trust that with dedication and perseverance, you can overcome them and deepen your God-consciousness.

Staying Motivated on the Path

Staying motivated on the path to God-consciousness can be a transformative and fulfilling journey. However, you have to undertake some strategies to help you stay motivated along the way. *First, you have to clarify your intention on why you seek God-*

consciousness and what it means to you personally. Clarify your intentions to yourself and the driving force behind your spiritual journey. Having a clear understanding of your motivations will provide a sense of direction and keep you focused on your path. When your intention is crystal clear, you can achieve your goal of the divine consciousness. Your goals must be specific, realistic, and meaningful goals that align with your spiritual aspirations.

Prepare a daily routine of daily spiritual practices that can nourish your connection with God. Be careful about your right timing and never violate the time slot. Daily spiritual practice may include prayer, meditation, and contemplation, reading spiritual texts, or engaging in acts of service. After some days of regular spiritual practice, you will be habituated to that time slot. If you fail any day performing regular practice, you will feel uncomfortable and feel guilty. Consistency in your practices will deepen your relationship with the divine and help you stay connected and motivated.

Some people may give you advice to get inspiration for the purpose. But remember self-motivation is the best option for spiritual growth. You may connect with the people of interest that resonate with your spiritual journey. Read books, listen to lectures or podcasts, listen to devotional music, or engage in spiritual conversations with like-minded individuals. Engage in spiritual gatherings and workshops. Participate in religious rituals where you can connect with others who are on a similar path. The support and encouragement of others can greatly motivate and inspire you.

Community prayer in churches, mosques, and temples are very useful examples in this context

Your life can't flourish without gratitude. Cultivate an attitude of gratitude for the blessings in your life and the experiences on your spiritual journey. ***Regularly acknowledge and appreciate the presence of the divine in your life. Yes, it is a fact that God is within you as a soul, (Atman) He is sitting in your heart. Recognize it gladly, your life will be full of blessings.*** Gratitude will uplift your spirits, enhance your connection with God, and keep you motivated. No doubt you may face some challenges on the path to God consciousness but never lose your heart. God may try to test your patience. Be firm on your journey and develop a resilient mindset. Take it as the blessing of God for further spiritual development.

Integrate the spiritual teachings into your daily life. As you deepen your understanding, strive to embody the principles and values you learn. Let your actions align with your spiritual beliefs and aspirations. The transformation in your own life can have a positive impact on others. Many may cite your example of transformation and you may be followed by many. In due course, you will able to build trust in your god. The growth and transformation will unfold in their own time and pace. Trust that the process is guiding you toward God consciousness. ***Patience and trust in the divine plan will keep you motivated and open to the unfolding of your spiritual path.*** Siridi SaiBaba, a Sadguru says-**"*śraddhā saburi*"**, where "śraddhā." means faith in god and *saburi* means patience. ***śraddhā saburi"*** is the guiding principle of the followers of SaiBaba.

Remember, motivation may fluctuate at times, but by incorporating these strategies into your life, you can stay inspired and connected on your path to God consciousness. Embrace the journey as an opportunity for growth, surrender to divine guidance, and trust in the transformative power of your spiritual practice.

Chapter Eight

The Importance of Community

The Role of Community in Spiritual Growth

We are social in our approaches, attitudes, values, and outlook, for which we need community support to grow in every space. Here also community plays a crucial role in our spiritual growth. It provides support, connection, and opportunities for learning and growth.

A spiritual community offers a support system that can uplift and inspire individuals on their spiritual journey. The community members share similar aspirations, challenges, and experiences. They create a safe space for individuals to seek guidance, share their struggles, and receive encouragement. This type of mental support helps individuals navigate obstacles, stay motivated, and focus on their journey to spiritual quests.

They often provide opportunities for shared learning and the exchange of wisdom. In group discussions, workshops, or study circles, community members can learn and understand better spiritual teachings, and explore different perspectives. Learning together in a community setting enhances spiritual growth by broadening one's knowledge and opening up new avenues for exploration. ***Shared rituals, ceremonies, or group meditations create a sacred space that amplifies spiritual vibrations and facilitates a deeper connection with the divine.*** The collective energy of the community supports individuals in accessing higher states of consciousness, experiencing profound spiritual insights, and cultivating a sense of unity and interconnectedness.

When you are part of a spiritual community your sense of accountability increases. In the ancient Indian Gurukul teaching system, such methods were introduced, where a prince and a village boy were treated equally and taught equally in the institutions. You might have heard Lord Krishna and Sudama (a poor Brahmin boy) studied together in the ashram of Rishi Sandipani. They were very good friends together. A sense of bonding and fellow feeling develops within the community that makes everyone grow together. The shared commitment and regular gatherings encourage individuals to stay consistent in their spiritual journey.

Community members developed a sense of accountability to provide support in maintaining a disciplined approach to spiritual growth. This accountability fosters commitment and dedication to personal transformation. However, you may not find everybody grows in the same space and dimension. Many may have made significant progress on their spiritual path. They can inspire and guide others in their journey. The community offer valuable insights, share their experiences, and provide guidance based on their spiritual practices and realizations. But remember in the path to spiritual realization, your Guru or spiritual teachers are the real treasure house of spiritual knowledge. They can provide the right path and direction on your journey. Having access to such mentors or gurus within the community accelerates spiritual growth and provides a roadmap for personal transformation.

Spiritual communities often emphasize service and acts of compassion. Engaging in service projects or community outreach programs allows individuals to apply their spiritual principles in practical ways. Serving others cultivates humility, compassion, and selfless contribution. The shared commitment to service strengthens the spiritual bond among community members and nurtures collective growth. Different religious groups or sects take different societal services to the poor and marginalized sections of society including cleaning of religious places like temples, churches, and mosques. Such a type of service not only increases awareness among the community members but also gives a message of selfless service to society.

When you are a part of a religious gathering, you might have felt the energy level of the united community. Celebrations of festive occasions within a spiritual community provide moments of joy, celebration, and gratitude. Coming together to acknowledge milestones, spiritual festivals, or personal achievements creates a sense of belonging and unity. These joyous occasions uplift the spirit, nurture a positive outlook, and remind individuals of the beauty and abundance of the spiritual path.

Community plays a vital role in spiritual growth by providing support, shared learning, accountability, opportunities for reflection, collective energy, and a space for service, collaboration, and celebration. Being part of a spiritual community nurtures personal growth, deepens the spiritual experience, and fosters a sense of connection and belonging on the journey toward self-realization and God-consciousness. Despite community participation, you may not get much-needed enlightenment unless you follow the teaching of your guru the spiritual guide with head and heart.

Finding Supportive Communities

Finding supportive communities in spiritual growth can be useful for your journey and provide the necessary support, guidance, and connection.

You can explore local spiritual centers, like churches, mosques, temples, or other places of worship that align with your spiritual beliefs. Attend their services, events, or gatherings to get a feel for the community and its teachings. Engage in conversations with community members and leaders to get the right people and environment to suit your spiritual growth.

You may connect the people online to meet your specific queries. Look for online groups, forums, or social media platforms that focus on your specific spiritual interests or teachings. Engage in discussions, share experiences, and seek guidance from like-minded individuals who can offer support and insights. But remember God realization is personal growth, which depends on your mindset, pursuit of knowledge, and intense longing for His blessings.

Many spiritual leaders regularly conduct discourses and deliver speeches in different forums. You may attend such types of practical classes to get practical guidance from them and get you motivated on your spiritual journey. Further, you can connect with participants and facilitators to establish connections that can extend beyond the event.

It is better to consider exploring meditation centers or yoga studios that offer classes, workshops, or group practices. These centers often attract individuals seeking personal growth, inner peace, and spiritual development. Your engagement in these practices within a supportive community can foster connections and provide a nurturing environment for your spiritual development and the calmness of your inner child.

You may find the recommendation of friends, who are aligned with spiritual growth useful in getting the right community that aligns with your values and aspirations. They may be aware of specific groups, teachers, or organizations that could be a good fit for you. Consider participating in spiritual retreats or embarking on pilgrimages to sacred sites associated with your spiritual tradition. These experiences often bring together individuals with a shared focus on spiritual growth and provide opportunities for deepening connections and forming supportive bonds with fellow seekers.

Once again, I can suggest seeking guidance from spiritual teachers, gurus, mentors, or guides who can offer personalized support and insights. Because I know what gurus mean to their disciples. They are invaluable assets to their disciples and the society. They can able to connect you with like-minded individuals or recommend specific communities that can support your spiritual growth. In Hinduism and Buddhism Gurus are true friends, philosophers, and guides of their disciples. They provide secret **Bija Mantras** to their disciples with specific instructions to recite, chant, or practice them. *Bija* mantras, also known as seed mantras, are single-syllable sounds or sacred syllables that hold spiritual and vibrational significance in various Eastern religious and spiritual traditions, particularly in Hinduism and Buddhism. The term *"bija"* in Sanskrit translates to **"seed"**, indicating that these mantras are considered the seeds of powerful spiritual energies.

Some popular *bija* mantras and their associated deities are:

1. *"Om" (Aum)*/ॐ - The most fundamental bija mantra, representing the cosmic sound or vibration.

2. ॐ ऐं ह्रीं क्लीं चामुण्डायै विच्चे/Om Aim Hrim Klim Chamundaye Viche/ "oṁ aiṁ hrīṁ klīṁ cāmuṇḍāyai vicce" - Associated with Goddess Durga.

3. *"oṁ gaṁ gaṇapataye namaḥ/* ॐ गं गणपतये नमः:- Associated with Lord Ganesha.

4. *"oṁ maṇi padme hūṁ"* - Associated with Avalokiteshvara (Bodhisattva of Compassion) in Buddhism.

When working with bija mantras, it is essential to do so with respect and understanding of their meanings and the spiritual context behind them. Chanting or meditating on bija mantras can be a powerful spiritual practice. But it is essential to carry out the instructions of your guru about its applications. You need sincerity and a pure heart to experience their full benefits. Additionally, proper pronunciation and guidance from gurus or spiritual teachers can be helpful when using bija mantras in spiritual practices.

When exploring these options, trust your intuition and choose communities that resonate with your values, beliefs, and aspirations. Take the time to observe the dynamics, energy, and teachings within the community to ensure they align with your spiritual path. Remember that finding a supportive community may require some exploration and trial-and-error, but the journey is worthwhile as you discover a Sadguru who can enhance your spiritual growth.

Navigating Challenges within Spiritual Communities

In our world, you may face challenges everywhere. Challenges make a man strong, perfect, and resilient. Likely spiritual communities can be a source of support and growth, but it is not devoid of challenges. You can have to pursue some strategies for navigating challenges within spiritual communities.

Not all teachings or practices may resonate with you, and it's important to ***trust your inner guidance.*** Evaluate the teachings and practices based on their alignment with your values, integrity, and spiritual well-being. Like a swan, you have to receive those teachings that align with your objective and enrich your values.

If you encounter a challenge or conflict within the community, approach it with a growth mindset. Reach out to the individual to seek understanding rather than judgment. Engage in open and respectful dialogue with them express your concerns and listen to their perspectives. This can foster communication, empathy, and the opportunity for resolution.

You may also see the diversity of beliefs and perspectives within the community. Spiritual communities often attract individuals with varying backgrounds and experiences. Embrace the opportunity to learn from different viewpoints and engage in respectful dialogues and discussions. But never lose your focus on core issues that align with your spiritual growth and understanding. For example, you are on the path of *bhakti* to realize God, where prayer, worship, and service to the guru are the basic concepts. If one community member says to practice meditation to achieve your true alignment, you should not follow that, at the expense of your regular practice because your path is different. Your guru or spiritual guide is there to assist you.

Setting boundaries in every space, and relationship is necessary. It is also applicable to our spiritual journey. Maintain healthy boundaries within the community to protect your well-being and maintain your personal growth. This may involve establishing boundaries around your time, energy, and involvement in community activities. Learn to say no when necessary and prioritize self-care to prevent burnout. Self-love is one of the priority sectors for enlightenment.

Embrace a mindset of compassion and forgiveness toward yourself and others within the community. ***Recognize that everyone is on their journey, and misunderstandings or conflicts may arise due to differing perspectives or conditioning.*** Cultivate compassion and forgiveness that can foster healing, harmony, and personal growth. Remember compassion and forgiveness are the stepping stones to your spiritual journey. They can expand your heart big enough to experience gratitude for your well-being and navigate challenges.

Stay focused on your own spiritual development, regardless of the challenges within the community. Nurture your practice, engage in self-reflection, and seek additional sources of spiritual inspiration outside the community if necessary. Never forget that your spiritual journey is ultimately an individual one, and you have the power to shape it. Remember your Sadguru or spiritual guide can provide all the answers to your excitement, queries, and inquisitions. If you find the spiritual guide not equipped enough to quench your thirst for knowledge for spiritual growth, then you may look for a better guide. But after all, you should continue respecting your spiritual guide and remain grateful to him. However, I can say from my personal experience, that a sadguru has every answer to any queries of his disciples. It is advised to get refuge in the lotus feet of your guru, the savior.

Remember that challenges within spiritual communities are opportunities for growth and learning. Approach them with an open heart, maintain integrity in your practice, and trust in your inner wisdom. By navigating challenges with grace and resilience, you can continue to grow and evolve on your spiritual path, whether within the community or beyond it. A guru or spiritual guide is supreme in navigating any spiritual issues and giving you specific direction.

Chapter Nine

Living a God-Conscious Life

Integrating Spiritual Practices into Daily Life

Integrating spiritual practices into daily life involves incorporating activities and beliefs that nourish your spiritual well-being into your everyday routine. It's about making spirituality an integral part of your life rather than keeping it for special occasions. When it is integrated with one's life, he sees the presence of God everywhere. Gita says,

विद्याविनयसंपन्ने ब्राह्मणे गवि हस्तिनि।
शुनि चैव श्वपाके च पण्डिताः समदर्शिनः॥ गीता ‖5.18‖

vidyā-vinaya-sampanne brāhmaṇe gavi hastini
śuni caiva śva-pāke ca paṇḍitāḥ sama-darśinaḥ

This verse emphasizes the qualities of *a wise and enlightened man* who is endowed with both knowledge and humility. Such a person sees all living beings through an equal lens irrespective of their social status or external appearances. Whether it is a learned Brahmin, a cow, an elephant, a dog, or even an outcast, a wise man sees the intrinsic value and divine essence in all living beings and treats them with equal respect and compassion. The verse encourages people to develop a broad and unbiased perspective and to cultivate a sense of oneness and empathy toward all creatures.

Mindfulness and Meditation:

Dedicate a few minutes each day to practice mindfulness or meditation. This involves focusing your attention on the present moment and observing your thoughts and feelings without judgment, which can help cultivate a sense of inner peace and clarity. You can follow a mindfulness meditation script with a focus on cultivating God consciousness or spiritual awareness:

Before you begin, find a quiet and comfortable place to sit or lie down. Take a few moments to relax and focus on your breathing to let go of any tension in your body.

Let's begin:

Close your eyes and take a few deep breaths. Inhale slowly and deeply through your nose, and exhale gently through your mouth. Allow yourself to become fully present in this moment. Take a moment to set your intention for this meditation. You may want to cultivate a deeper connection with God, the divine, or your higher self. Open your heart to the presence of divine love and wisdom.

Bring your attention to your breath. Notice the sensation of the air entering and leaving your nostrils, or the rise and fall of your abdomen. As you breathe in, imagine that you are breathing in divine energy and love. As you breathe out, you feel that all worries, negative energies, or distractions are leaving your body and mind. You are feeling very relaxed now. If it resonates with you, you can use a mantra to deepen your connection with God-consciousness. You can silently repeat a sacred word or phrase with each breath, such as *"God is love," "Om," "Divine presence,"* or any other mantra that feels meaningful to you. If you have a guru in your life, you can silently recite the *guru mantra.*

Now, visualize a radiant and loving light at the center of your being. This light represents the divine presence within you. See it growing brighter with each breath, expanding and filling your entire body with divine energy. Imagine this divine light expanding beyond your body, connecting you with the entire universe. Feel a sense of unity with all living beings, knowing that the same divine presence exists within each of them.

Let go of any thoughts or distractions that may arise. If your mind starts to wander, gently bring your focus back to the divine light and your breath. Surrender any worries, fears, or doubts to the divine presence, trusting in its wisdom and love. Take a moment to express gratitude for this sacred time of connection. Feel the love and peace that comes from being in the presence of God-consciousness. Bask in this divine light and allow it to fill you with joy, happiness, and serenity.

After a few minutes when you feel ready, gently open your eyes. Carry the sense of God consciousness with you throughout your day, knowing that you can always return to this sacred space of mindfulness and connection. You can start the meditation with a few minutes and gradually increase it to ten to fifteen minutes to get better results.

Remember, the practice of mindfulness meditation with a focus on God consciousness is a personal and spiritual journey. Each session may be different, and it's okay to have varying experiences. ***Approach this practice with an open heart and a sense of reverence, knowing that the divine presence is always within and around you. He is here to help you and uplift you and is very kind to watch you and inspire you from within. Believe Him, rest is His task.***

Gratitude Practice:

Expression of gratitude is a powerful spiritual practice. Take time each day to reflect on the things you are grateful for and write them down or share them with others. This often helps shift your focus to the positive aspects of your divine life and cultivates a sense of appreciation. Gratitude practice is a beautiful way to deepen your connection with God consciousness.

Before you begin, find a quiet and comfortable space where you are free of disturbance. You may sit in a cross-legged position or lie down, whichever is more comfortable for you. You can do the practice in the early morning or evening as per your time slot.

Let's Begin:

Take a few deep breaths to center yourself and bring your awareness to the present moment. Inhale deeply through your nose, hold for a moment, and then exhale slowly through your mouth. Feel that all your tension is leaving your body and mind with each breath out.

Visualize a radiant light at the center of your chest, your **heart chakra.** This light represents the divine presence within you. Imagine it growing bright to brighter and warm to warmer with each breath, filling your entire being with love and compassion.

Bring to mind the blessings in your life, both big and small. These blessings could be aspects of your life, experiences, relationships, opportunities, or anything that you are grateful for. Take a moment to appreciate and acknowledge each one.

With each blessing that comes to mind, express your gratitude to the divine. You can say silently or out loud, *"Thank you, dear God (or any other name you use for the divine), for the gift of [name the blessing]. I am truly grateful."* As you express your gratitude, feel the presence of the divine surrounding you. Imagine the love and light of God consciousness embracing you, filling you with a sense of peace and contentment.

Along with blessings, bring to mind any challenges or difficult experiences you've faced. Recognize that even these challenges have valuable lessons and growth opportunities hidden within them. Offer thanks for the wisdom gained and the strength to overcome them. Acknowledge and appreciate how each experience, both positive and negative, has contributed to your spiritual growth and evolution. Recognize that everything serves a purpose on your soul's journey.

Now, expand your gratitude beyond your personal life. Offer thanks for the beauty of nature, the support of loved ones, and the countless blessings bestowed upon humanity. Embrace a sense of interconnectedness with all living beings. Allow yourself to bask in the feeling of gratitude and divine love. Stay in this space for a few moments, soaking in the blessings and the presence of God-consciousness.

When you're ready to conclude the practice, take a few deep breaths and gently open your eyes. Carry this sense of gratitude and connection with you throughout your day.

Remember, gratitude is a powerful practice that can transform your perspective and cultivate a deeper sense of love and appreciation for life's blessings. Make time for this meditation regularly, and you'll likely find that your sense of God consciousness and spiritual awareness deepens over time.

Daily Reflection or Journaling:

Set aside time each day for self-reflection or journaling. Use this time to explore your thoughts, emotions, and experiences, and gain deeper insights into yourself and your spiritual journey.

Connection with Nature:

Nature is a big inspiration and a great healer for all. It gives positive energy taking negativity from us. Spend time in nature regularly, whether it's going for a walk in the park, gardening, or simply sitting outside and observing the natural world. Listen to the different melodious voices of the birds and watch their flights and expansions of their wings, you can be mused. See the beautiful decorated sky with floating clouds, a beautiful sunrise or sunset. Your connection with nature can be a deeply spiritual experience and helps foster a sense of interconnectedness with the world around you.

Rituals and Ceremonies:

Make everyday personal rituals or ceremonies that are part and parcel of the spiritual journey that holds meaning for you. These can be as simple as lighting a candle, reciting mantras, performing puja, singing a devotional song, or a prayer. It may also include offering water to the Sun god, watering a basil plant (Tulsi), or performing a symbolic gesture to mark a transition or honor something significant in your life that aligns with your belief system.

Engaging in Acts of Kindness and Service:

Practicing compassion and serving others is an essential aspect of almost all spiritual traditions. Find ways to render selfless service to others, whether through volunteering, helping a friend in need, or performing random acts of kindness. Practice kindness in your attitude and approaches toward self and others.

Compassion and kindness are two precious heavenly qualities, liked by God. Different holy scriptures have figured out different fables and stories to create awareness in the hearts of humans about kindness and selfless services. These qualities cultivate a sense of connection with the divine and serve the purpose of fulfillment.

Study and Contemplation:

You must engage in reading sacred books of your beliefs. Study sacred texts like the Bhagavad Gita, the Bible, or the Quran, or explore philosophical and metaphysical concepts that resonate with you. *Take time to contemplate and integrate these teachings into your life. Unless your learning is reflected in your life, your learning is incomplete and your objective is unfulfilled.*

Remember, integrating spiritual practices into daily life is a personal journey. If you are serious about your spiritual journey, you must follow the instructions meticulously. However, it's essential to find what resonates with you. Experiment with different practices, be patient with yourself and allow your spirituality to evolve and unfold naturally over time.

Developing a Deeper Understanding of the Divine in Daily Life

Developing a deeper understanding of the divine in daily life involves cultivating a sense of connection and relationship with a higher power or a transcendent source of meaning. It is about recognizing and experiencing the presence of the divine in all aspects of life.

Approach each day with an openness and receptivity to the divine. Cultivate an attitude of reverence, gratitude, and awe toward the world around you. Start your day with a prayer-

सर्वेभवन्तु सुखिनः।
सर्वेसन्तु निरामयाः।
सर्वेभद्राणि पश्यन्तु।
मा कश्चिद्दुःखभाग्भवेत्॥

Sarvebhavantu sukhinaḥ.
Sarvesantu nirāmayāḥ.
Sarvebhadraṇi paśyantu.
Mā kashchidduḥkhabhāgbhavet.

This mantra is a prayer for the well-being and happiness of all living beings. It expresses the wish for the welfare and prosperity of everyone, with a compassionate heart and the desire for the elimination of suffering. By chanting or reciting this mantra, one sends positive intentions and vibrations to all beings, promoting peace, prosperity, love, and harmony in the world. See every moment and every experience as an opportunity to connect with something greater than yourself.

Try to quiet your mind, and listen to the inner wisdom and guidance of the divine. This can be done through **meditation, prayer**, or simply finding a peaceful place where you can reflect and contemplate. Good thoughts can appear in your mind when you are calm and quiet. Pay attention to synchronicities, coincidences, and meaningful signs that occur in your life. These can be seen as messages or communications from the divine. Reflect on their significance and how they might be guiding you on your spiritual path. Incorporate spiritual practices, rituals, and ceremonies into your daily routine. These can vary depending on your beliefs and traditions as discussed earlier.

Engage yourself in spiritual study and exploration to deepen your understanding of the divine. This can involve reading sacred texts and studying the teachings of spiritual leaders or philosophers. You can attend lectures, workshops, or discourses of spiritual leaders and participate in discussions or study groups. Expand your knowledge and broaden your perspectives to gain new insights into the nature of the divine.

Reflect on your personal experiences and moments of transcendence. *Look for the presence of the divine in moments of joy, love, and beauty, and even in times of challenge and adversity*. Consider how these experiences shape your understanding of the divine and how they inform your spiritual journey. Recognize and honor the interconnectedness of all beings and the web of life. See the divine not only in yourself but in others, in nature, and the world around you. Practice compassion, kindness, and empathy toward all living beings, knowing that they too are expressions of the divine. Practice *"Jibe Daya."* This means *"Have compassion for all living beings"* in English.

The concept of *"Jibe Daya"* is deeply rooted in many spiritual and philosophical traditions. It emphasizes the importance of compassion and empathy as essential qualities for leading a meaningful and harmonious life. By practicing "jibe daya," individuals strive to treat others with kindness, love, and respect, fostering a sense of interconnectedness and contributing to well-being. Further, develop trust in your inner guidance and intuition. *The divine often communicates with us through our intuition, offering insights and guidance. Learn to listen to your inner voice and discern the wisdom it imparts.*

It is mentioned earlier that developing a deeper understanding of the divine is a personal and ongoing process. It requires patience, openness, and a willingness to explore the possibilities. Your intention, eagerness, and love for the divine are the stepping stones on your journey. Allow your understanding to evolve and expand as you deepen your connection with the divine in your daily life.

Maintaining a Connection with the Divine Amidst Life's Challenges

Somebody says- ***"Hope for the best but prepare for the worst."*** This is one of the important chapters of your life lesson. On the path to God consciousness, you may face something challenging. However, you should not stop there. Maintaining a connection with the divine amidst life's challenges can be a source of strength, comfort, and reward. There are some ways to nurture and sustain that connection during difficult times.

The most powerful mediums to seek solace and guidance from the divine are *prayer or meditation* practices. These practices can help calm the mind, cultivate inner peace, and provide a space for you to express your concerns, fears, and hopes. They allow you to connect with a higher power and surrender your worries to something greater than yourself. When you find someone to get refuge with, then your concerns, fears, and apprehensions are no longer left with you. Now you are free, responsibilities are shifted to your divine power. Practice trust and surrender in the face of challenges before Him with a prayer-"सरणागत मां जगदीश रक्ष" ***"O Lord of the Universe, protect me from all the obstacles as I seek refuge in you."*** Trust that there is a divine plan unfolding and that you are being supported even in difficult times. Develop unwavering faith in Him, and remember the divine is guiding you toward growth and transformation.

You may find a spiritual community with like-minded individuals who share your spiritual beliefs and values. You can get strength and inspiration from the spiritual teachings, discourses, and wisdom that resonate with you. Reflect on passages from sacred texts, inspirational quotes, or teachings from your guru or spiritual leaders that offer guidance and perspective. Use these teachings as a source of comfort and guidance during challenging times.

Never forget to cultivate gratitude even amid difficulties. During such an uncomfortable time you must offer gratitude to God. Remember the situation may have been aggravated, without the intervention of the divine in your sufferings. Be grateful for His big planning for you. Find things to be grateful for, no matter how small, and acknowledge the blessings in your life. This helps shift your focus from problems to the positive aspects, fostering resilience and strengthening your connection with the divine.

Learn the lessons from the challenges you face. Make the challenges as opportunities for growth, learning, or spiritual development. Trust that the divine has a purpose in every experience and that even in difficult times, there is something to be gained.

Serving others can be a powerful way to maintain a connection with the divine amidst challenges as mentioned earlier. You may also donate in cash or kind to the needy. Engage in acts of kindness and compassion. Extending love and care to others, means extending love and care to God and you align yourself with the divine.

But you should not forget or neglect your health or emotional issues. Take care of your physical, emotional, and spiritual health. Nurture your well-being through practices that recharge and replenish you. Treat yourself with kindness, understanding, and self-compassion. Recognize that you deserve love and care. Believe in yourself for spiritual growth and fulfillment.

Moreover, to keep maintaining a connection with the divine during challenging times is a testing period. No doubt it is a personal journey, and different approaches may resonate with different individuals. Trust your intuition and follow the path that brings you closer to the divine and supports your well-being as suggested in the chapter.

Chapter Ten

Conclusion

Reflections on the Journey to God Consciousness

The journey to God consciousness is a profound and transformative process of self-discovery and spiritual awakening. It involves a deepening awareness of the divine within and around us, and an ongoing quest to connect with the ultimate reality or God. Journey to God consciousness is different from your journey to achieve specific materialistic goals in many aspects. You can manipulate many things to achieve success in the physical world but you can't do that in the spiritual arena. You have to involve your pure heart and devotion to achieve unlimited success in this journey.

The journey to God consciousness begins with self-exploration. It involves delving into the depths of your being, questioning your beliefs, and examining your thoughts, emotions, and behaviors. By understanding and accepting yourself, you pave the way for a deeper connection with the divine.

This journey is about a search for truth. It involves questioning and seeking answers to life's existential questions. It requires an open mind and a willingness to explore various spiritual traditions, philosophies, and teachings. As you seek truth, you develop a broader perspective and gain insights that guide you toward a deeper understanding of the divine.

The first principle of this journey is total surrender to a higher power and embrace humility. When you realize that there is a power greater than yourself and relinquish the need for control allows you to open up to the divine and experience a sense of surrender. ***Humility enables you to acknowledge that you are part of something much larger and interconnected system.***

It is a transformative process that leads to your inner growth and evolution. As you deepen your connection with the divine, you become more aware of your shortcomings and strive to overcome them. This involves cultivating virtues such as love, compassion, forgiveness, and gratitude, and letting go of negative patterns and attachments that hinder your spiritual progress. You have to understand that the journey to God consciousness is not limited to meditation or religious rituals alone. It encompasses recognizing and experiencing the presence of the divine in every aspect of life. It is about perceiving the sacredness in the ordinary, finding beauty in nature, and connecting with the divine through acts of kindness, service, and love. As you progress on the journey to God consciousness, you begin to recognize the inherent unity and interconnectedness of all beings and the world. You see beyond the superficial differences created by humans and divisions and perceive the underlying unity that binds everything together. This awareness leads to a deeper sense of compassion, empathy, and harmony. It also involves realizing that the divine is not separate from you but resides within your being. It is an inner awakening, a recognition of your divine essence. This realization leads to a profound shift in your perception of yourself and others, fostering a sense of unity and divine love.

You have to admit in your **mind and heart** that the journey to God consciousness is an ongoing process that unfolds throughout your life, even for different incarnations. It is not a destination but a continuous exploration and expansion of your spiritual awareness. Embrace the idea that you are forever evolving and that your connection with the divine deepens with each step you take.

Further, it is needless to mention that, the journey to God consciousness is unique for each individual. Embrace your path, trust yourself and your intuition, and be open to the guidance and revelations that come along the way. It is a transformative and deeply fulfilling journey that leads to a profound connection with the divine and a greater sense of purpose and fulfillment in life.

Future Steps on the Path to God Consciousness

Now you are clear that the path to God consciousness is a lifelong journey, and can go beyond your present incarnation. But you can take some potential future steps to keep you in the right direction of spiritual alignment.

Explore and deepen your existing spiritual practices or incorporate new ones into your routine. This could involve dedicating more time to meditation, prayer, contemplation, or engaging in specific rituals that resonate with your spiritual path. Experiment with different techniques or traditions to find what nourishes your soul and deepens your connection with the divine.

Cultivate a deeper sense of inner peace and silence. Set aside regular periods for silence and solitude, allowing yourself to be fully present in the present moment. In this space of stillness, you can cultivate a greater receptivity to the divine and a heightened awareness of its presence.

When confused never hesitate to seek guidance from your guru, spiritual mentors, or spiritual communities that resonate with your path. Connect with individuals who have walked a similar journey or possess deep spiritual wisdom. Their guidance can provide insights, support, and inspiration as you continue to navigate the path to God consciousness.

Be consistent and dive deeper into the study of sacred texts, spiritual literature, and teachings that align with your beliefs. Engage in reflective reading, contemplation, and dialogue with others to gain a deeper understanding of the divine principles and insights shared in these texts. Allow their wisdom to inform and guide your journey and leave them to reflect on your daily activities. Embrace opportunities to expand your worldview and explore diverse spiritual traditions and philosophies. Attend workshops, seminars, or retreats that expose you to different spiritual perspectives and practices. This can broaden your understanding of the divine and help you integrate various aspects into your spiritual path.

Focus on developing virtues and qualities that align with the divine. Cultivate compassion, love, kindness, forgiveness, and humility in your interactions with others and yourself. Practice selfless service and acts of kindness to extend the divine presence in your daily life. Deepen your practice of surrender and letting go. Release attachments, expectations, and the need for control, trusting in the divine plan. Surrender to the flow of life and have faith that the divine is guiding and supporting you even in uncertain times. Let your spirituality infuse your thoughts, words, actions, and relationships. Cultivate mindfulness, presence, and awareness in all that you do, seeing the divine in every moment and every being.

Remember, you are a unique child of the god. Trust your inner guidance, be open to new experiences and insights, and remain committed to the continuous growth and deepening of your spiritual connection with the divine.

Encouragement to Continue the Journey to God Consciousness

In Hindu bhakti philosophy and God consciousness, Krishna Consciousness is very popular. In Krishna consciousness, Sri Rādhā is the consort of Lord Krishna. Her love for Krishna is a bright example of God-consciousness. Now you may be excited to know the pattern or nature of the love of Rādhā. In her perception of love, wherever she sees only sees Krishna everywhere. The entire universe is only filled by Krishna. He is present in the sky, air, fire, earth, stars, planets, living and non-living. Further, when she closes her eyes, she meets Krishna in her own heart. Now you are sure what the real God consciousness is. You have to rise to the level of "Rādhā.", awakening the *"Rādhābhāba."* within you.

Continuing the journey to God consciousness is a beautiful and worthwhile endeavor. It offers a profound sense of fulfillment and purpose. As you deepen your connection with the divine, you experience a deep sense of inner peace, joy, and harmony. This spiritual fulfillment transcends fleeting external circumstances, providing a lasting source of contentment and meaning in life. Embracing the journey to God consciousness opens you up to an expanded perspective of reality. You begin to see beyond the limitations of the physical world and perceive the interconnectedness and oneness of all things. This broader perspective can bring clarity, wisdom, and a deep sense of awe and wonder.

It is a transformative process that facilitates personal growth and evolution. As you engage in spiritual practices, reflect on your experiences, and cultivate virtues, you become more aligned with your higher self. This transformation impacts all areas of your life, enhancing your relationships, well-being, and overall sense of fulfillment.

When you deepen your connection with the divine that allows you to tap into the wellspring of unconditional love and compassion within you. As you grow in God consciousness, you develop an immense capacity to love and show compassion toward yourself and others. ***This love and compassion become a powerful force for healing and positive change in the world. You can realize that you are not alone. The divine is always there, providing guidance, support, and inspiration along the way. Every work is being done automatically without any obstacles or outside support.***

There is a story from the life of an Indian saint. Once he invited some guests to a feast in his hermitage. However, subsequently, he forgets the invitation. When he realized and recalled the invitation, it was very late, he became ashamed and rushed to the spot of occurrence. However, a big surprise was waiting for him. Guests were very happy to grace the occasion and highly appreciated the saint and his hospitality. Then who has performed the duties of the saint, the question may arise in everybody's mind. The answer is the entire responsibility was shoulder by God himself in the guise of the saint. Now I feel you are clear about the real scenario of God consciousness. Cultivating a receptive heart and mind, you can tap into this divine grace and guidance.

Further, as you deepen your connection with the divine, you also deepen your connection with others. The journey to God consciousness fosters empathy, understanding, and a genuine appreciation for the interconnectedness of all beings. It allows you to cultivate harmonious relationships based on love, respect, and compassion, creating a more compassionate and inclusive world. God consciousness infuses your life with profound meaning and purpose. It helps you uncover the deeper significance of your existence and understand your unique role in the divine plan. This awareness brings clarity to your life's purpose and empowers you to contribute your gifts and talents in service to others and the greater good.

It also reminds you of the eternal nature of your soul. It deepens your understanding that life extends beyond the physical realm and that your spiritual essence is timeless and eternal. This realization brings comfort, strength, and a sense of immortality amidst the transient nature of the material world. Trust in the divine guidance and wisdom that unfolds along the way. No doubt your journey to God consciousness is on the right track. Follow the instructions of your guru, or spiritual teachers for spiritual growth, profound connection, and a transformative realization of the divine within and around you. Continue your journey to the horizon of divine abundance.

Key Takeaways from the Book

God *Consciousness Definition:* God consciousness is an elevated awareness of a profound connection with the divine, transcending cultural boundaries and recognizing unity in all existence.

Key Aspects: Unity and Interconnectedness, Transcendence of Ego, and Divine Presence are central aspects, emphasizing oneness and omnipresence.

Importance of Divine Connection: Seeking a divine connection satisfies the human longing for spiritual fulfillment, provides guidance, offers love and support, and establishes a moral framework.

Role of Religion: Religion offers structured practices, moral guidance, community support, and sacred texts, acting as a framework for spiritual growth and God consciousness.

Chapter-2

Diverse Beliefs: Various beliefs about God exist across cultures and religions, ranging from monotheism (Judaism, Christianity, Islam) to polytheism (Greek mythology, Hinduism), pantheism (Spinoza, Advaita Vedanta), atheism (Dawkins, Hitchens), agnosticism (Huxley, Russell), and deism (Jefferson).

Scientific Perspective: Science, while successful in explaining the natural world, cannot empirically prove or disprove the existence of God. Arguments for God's existence, such as the cosmological or teleological arguments, are philosophical and not scientifically verifiable.

Coexistence of Science and Spirituality: Many scientists find no conflict between scientific work and personal beliefs in God, acknowledging that science and spirituality address different aspects of understanding and meaning.

Nature of God: Across diverse beliefs, God is described as both transcendent and immanent, with attributes like omnipotence and omniscience. The Bhagavad Gita and the Hebrew Bible illustrate omnipresence. God is often seen as the creator, and some perceive Him personally while others see an impersonal force.

Role of Faith: Faith and spirituality provide meaning, ethical frameworks, and personal growth. They foster connections with the divine, support the community, and offer resources for coping with challenges. The role of faith is deeply personal, it influences beliefs, values, and individual experiences of transcendence.

Chapter-3

The Essence of Self: The chapter delves into the profound question of *"Who am I?"* emphasizing the immortal nature of the self (Atman) as declared in Eastern philosophies. It explores the relationship between self-awareness and God consciousness, highlighting the importance of understanding one's true nature beyond the illusions of the ego.

Self-awareness as a Path: Self-awareness is presented as a transformative journey toward God consciousness. It involves the dissolution of the ego, recognition of the divine within, understanding interconnectedness, and experiencing an integration of the self with the divine.

Tools for Cultivating Self-awareness: Practical tools like mindfulness meditation, journaling, self-reflection, feedback from others, emotional awareness, body awareness, and retreats are offered as effective means for developing self-awareness. Overcoming obstacles, such as denial and comparison, is discussed, emphasizing the importance of persistence and self-compassion in the lifelong process of self-discovery and spiritual awareness.

Chapter-4

Meditation Techniques: Embrace mindfulness, loving-kindness, transcendental, visualization, chakra, and yoga meditation for stress reduction, improved focus, emotional well-being, and a connection with a higher power.

Power of Prayer: Understand prayer's significance in energy transfer, expressing gratitude, seeking guidance, and fostering a personal connection with the divine. Types include adoration, supplication, intercession, contemplative, and confession prayers.

Contemplation and Mindfulness: Engage in intentional reflection, non-judgmental observation, and contemplative practices for enhanced self-awareness, inner peace, expanded perspectives, emotional well-being, and spiritual growth. Explore mindfulness to deepen your connection with the divine, drawing inspiration from diverse religious traditions.

Chapter-5

- Gratitude, rooted in deep appreciation, transforms life's challenges into opportunities, fostering spiritual growth and resilience. It aligns us with God's purpose, cultivating humility, trust, and faith.
- Gratitude positively impacts emotional well-being, relationships, and physical health. It counters materialism, inspires generosity, and enhances mindfulness, connecting us with God through sincere practice.
- Practical tips include keeping a gratitude journal, morning practices, expressing thanks, mindful walks, gratitude meditation, mealtime reflections, and bedtime gratitude, fostering a continuous and transformative gratitude mindset.

Chapter-6

The Power of Love in Spiritual Growth: Love, as described in Corinthians 13:4-7, is transformative, fostering compassion, unity, gratitude, and connection with the divine. It heals, transcends dualities, and integrates wisdom, leading to inner transformation, fulfillment, and joy in the spiritual journey.

Loving Oneself in God Consciousness: Recognizing the divine within, practicing self-acceptance, cultivating inner harmony, and expressing divine love contribute to spiritual growth. It involves aligning with one's true nature and radiating love to enrich both self and others.

Loving Others and God Consciousness: Loving others intertwine with God-consciousness, guided by spiritual teachings. Acts of love, service, and unity cultivate a compassionate existence, reflecting a deeper connection to a higher power and spiritual reality.

Compassion and Empathy in Spiritual Growth: Compassion and empathy promote oneness, self-reflection, healing, forgiveness, altruism, and an expanded consciousness. These qualities open the heart, integrate spiritual teachings, and strengthen the connection with the divine, contributing to profound spiritual growth.

Chapter-7

- Overcoming obstacles to God consciousness involves addressing common challenges like ego identification, attachment, lack of self-awareness, distractions, negative conditioning, and more.
- Strategies for overcoming obstacles include self-reflection, mindfulness, surrender, prayer, the study of spiritual texts, seeking guidance, cultivating virtuous qualities, serving others, and practicing gratitude.
- Staying motivated on the path requires clarifying intentions, setting realistic goals, establishing a daily routine, seeking inspiration, fostering community connections, expressing gratitude, and integrating spiritual teachings into daily life with patience and trust in the divine plan.

Chapter-8

Community's Role in Spiritual Growth: Spiritual communities offer support, shared learning, accountability, and opportunities for service, collaboration, and celebration. Being part of a community nurtures personal growth, deepens spiritual experiences, and fosters a sense of connection and belonging on the journey to self-realization and God-consciousness.

Finding Supportive Communities: Seek supportive communities aligned with your spiritual beliefs through local centers, online groups, meditation/yoga studios, and recommendations from friends or spiritual leaders. Engage in discussions, attend events, and explore various avenues to find a community that resonates with your values and aspirations.

Navigating Challenges: Practice discernment, seek understanding, embrace differences, set boundaries, and cultivate compassion and forgiveness when navigating challenges within spiritual communities. Focus on personal growth, stay true to your path, and remember that challenges are opportunities for learning and evolution on your spiritual journey.

Chapter-9

Integrating Spiritual Practices: Incorporate mindfulness, meditation, gratitude, daily reflection, connection with nature, rituals, and acts of kindness into your routine for a God-conscious life.

Deeper Understanding of the Divine: Cultivate a spiritual mindset, engage in study and contemplation, reflect on personal experiences, and recognize the divine in daily life to deepen your understanding of the divine.

Maintaining Connection Amid Challenges: Use prayer, meditation, community support, gratitude, and self-care to sustain your connection with the divine during life's challenges, trusting in a higher purpose and learning from difficult experiences.

Chapter-10

Journey to God Consciousness: A transformative self-discovery, requiring self-exploration, humility, and cultivating virtues. Recognizing the divine in every aspect of life leads to inner growth, unity, and compassion.

Future Steps: Deepen spiritual practices, embrace silence, seek guidance, study sacred texts, and cultivate virtues. Stay consistent, open-minded, and mindful, recognizing the lifelong and evolving nature of the journey.

Encouragement: Embracing God consciousness brings lasting fulfillment, clarity, love, and compassion. It transforms personal growth, enhances relationships, and connects you to a deeper purpose, emphasizing the eternal nature of the soul.

Disclaimer

This book is for educational purposes only. Readers acknowledge that the author does not render legal, financial, medical, or professional advice. The content within this book has been derived from various sources. Please consult a licensed professional before attempting any techniques outlined in this book.

By reading this document, the reader agrees that under no circumstances is the author responsible for any direct or indirect losses incurred as a result of the use of the information contained within this document, including but not limited to errors, omissions, or inaccuracies.

Adherence to all applicable laws and regulations, including international, federal, state, and local governing professional licensing, business practices, advertising, and all other jurisdictions, is the sole responsibility of the purchaser or reader.

Neither the author nor the publisher assumes any responsibility or liability whatsoever on behalf of the purchaser or reader of these materials. Any perceived slight of any individual or organization is purely unintentional.

May I Ask You for a Small Favor?

At the outset, I want to give a big thanks for taking out time to read this book. You could have chosen any other book, but you chose mine, and I totally appreciate this.

I hope you got at least a few actionable insights that will have a positive impact on your day-to-day life.

Can I ask for 30 seconds more of your time?

I would love it if you could leave a review about the book. Reviews may not matter to big-name authors; but they're a tremendous help for authors like me, who don't have many followers. They help me grow my readership by encouraging folks to take a chance on my books.

To put it straight, reviews are the lifeblood of any author.

"The Path to God Consciousness"

Please leave your review by visiting the "**Review Section** "of this book's page.

It will just take less than a minute of your time, but will tremendously help me to reach out to more people, so please leave your review.

Thanks for your support of my work. And I would love to see your review.